REEDS SKIPPER'S HANDBOOK

FOR SAIL AND POWER

Sixth edition

MALCOLM PEARSON
RYA Yachtmaster Instructor

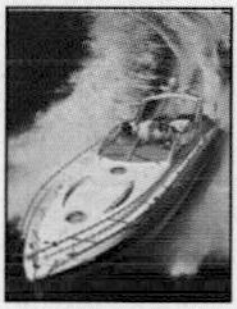

ADLARD COLES NAUTICAL
LONDON

Dedicated to Jack – my evening star.
May he never lose his way.

And Major – *safe in harbour now.*

Published by Adlard Coles Nautical
an imprint of A & C Black (Publishers) Ltd
36 Soho Square, London W1D 3QY
www.adlardcoles.com

First edition published by Thomas Reed Publications 1993
Second edition 1995
Revised 1998
Third edition 2000
Reprinted 2002
Fourth edition published by Adlard Coles Nautical 2004
Fifth edition 2007
Sixth edition 2010

ISBN 978-1-4081-2477-2

A CIP catalogue record for this book is available from the British Library.

Typeset in Myriad Light 9/11 pt by Margaret Brain
Original drawings by Sherrie Pearson;
Illustrations by Barbara McGavin and Dave Saunders

Printed and bound in Singapore by Star Standard.

CONTENTS

Introduction

First published in 1993, *Reeds Skipper's Handbook* soon became a nautical best seller. It is now sold worldwide and appears in several foreign language editions. This 6th edition has been revised and updated to include useful extra information on tides, chart plotting, boat handling and knots plus a new section on sails and wind.

GPS and electronic chart plotters have significantly affected the way we navigate and made it possible for us to fix our position with greater accuracy than ever before. As a consequence, though, there is a danger that some skippers might become so reliant on their 'electronics' that they forget how to navigate effectively without them. Of course, the electronic device that is guaranteed never to malfuntion has yet to be invented so it is unwise to neglect the traditional skills that will get you home safely if your GPS fails. *Reeds Skipper's Handbook* is designed to explain the basics of 'traditional navigation' and seamanship in simple terms, and solutions to most of the problems that are likely to occur during a coastal passage can be quickly found within its pages.

Malcolm Pearson

Acknowledgements

In recognition of the leading part played by the RYA in the promotion of safe practice for recreational boaters, it should be noted that many of the techniques explained in this book emanate from the RYA and are those routinely taught by RYA trained instructors to students enrolled on their navigation and seamanship courses.

The figures on pages 11, 33, 34, 35, 71, 76, 79 and 83 are based upon or are reproduced from Admiralty Charts or publications with permission from The Controller of Her Majesty's Stationery Office and the UK Hydrographic Office.

The Life Saving Signals on pages 128–9 are based upon material issued by the MCA and are reproduced with their kind permission.

Thanks to *Practical Boat Owner* for permission to reproduce material previously published in that magazine.

Finally, my special thanks to my wife Sherrie without whose help and artistic ability this book would not have been published.

NOTE: Every effort has been made to find the copyright holders of any material used in this book that is not the author's own.

Latitude and longitude

Latitude and longitude

The network of imaginary lines seen on a globe of the world is used to define position on its surface. The horizontal lines are *parallels of latitude* and the vertical lines that converge at the poles are *meridians of longitude* (*Fig 1*).

Latitude is measured vertically along a meridian from 0° to 90° either north or south of the Equator (*Fig 2*).

Longitude is measured horizontally round the equator from 0° to 180° either east or west of the Greenwich Meridian (*Fig 3*).

- Lines of latitude and longitude form complete circles around the globe. There are 360° in a circle and each degree can be divided into 60 minutes.
- Using these co-ordinates, any place on Earth can be precisely defined as a position of latitude and longitude.
- Traditionally, latitude is always given first followed by longitude and in coastal navigation, position is usually defined to the nearest minute, or if greater accuracy is required, tenths of a minute can also be quoted, ie:
  Bishop Rock 49° 52´.3N 006° 26´.7W

Mercator projection

To portray the global Earth on a flat chart a projection called Mercator is generally used. As with a globe, charts are also overprinted with a lattice of latitude and longitude but on a Mercator chart, the meridians are drawn parallel to each other. Doing this distorts the landmasses in an east-west direction so to preserve the shape of the land, the north-south distance between successive parallels of latitude is progressively increased in proportion toward each pole.

Latitude and longitude

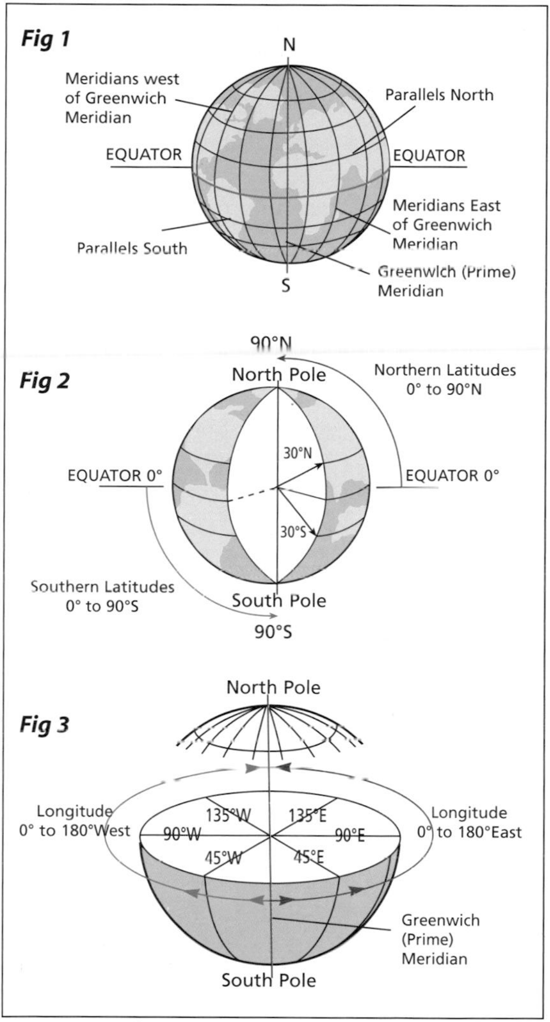

Mercator charts

Mercator charts and rhumb Lines

The real value of Mercator's projection is that although the scale of the landmasses is distorted, direction is unaffected. This means that a straight line drawn between any two positions on a Mercator chart will cross every meridian at the same angle, so the navigator has only to measure that angle to obtain the true course to follow from one position to the other (*Fig 4*).

A line that crosses all meridians at the same angle is called a *rhumb line*.

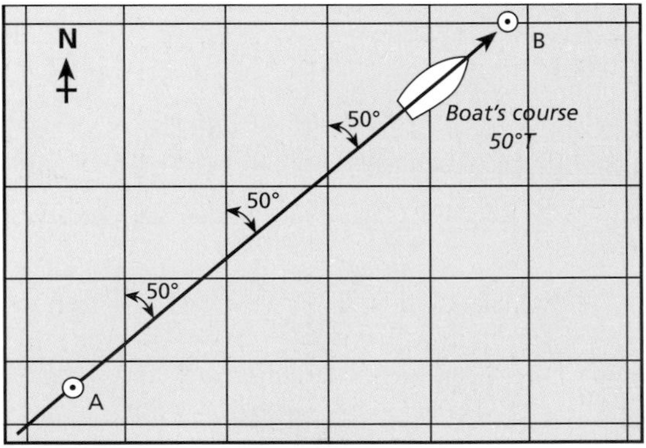

Fig 4

The rhumb line course between two points is not, however, the shortest distance between them, this is only given by a Great Circle route, but for coastal and offshore passages of less than five or six hundred miles in low or middle latitudes, the difference is negligible and can be safely disregarded.

Great circles and gnomonic charts

A **Great Circle** is the largest circle that can be drawn on the surface of the Earth, and the shortest distance between any two points on the surface lies along the arc of a Great Circle that passes through them both.

A **Gnomonic chart** portrays meridians as straight lines that converge toward the nearest pole. Parallels, other than the Equator, appear as curves.

Gnomonic charts are commonly used to plan long ocean voyages because a Great Circle route can be drawn on a chart as a straight line between the departure point and the intended destination (*Fig 5*).

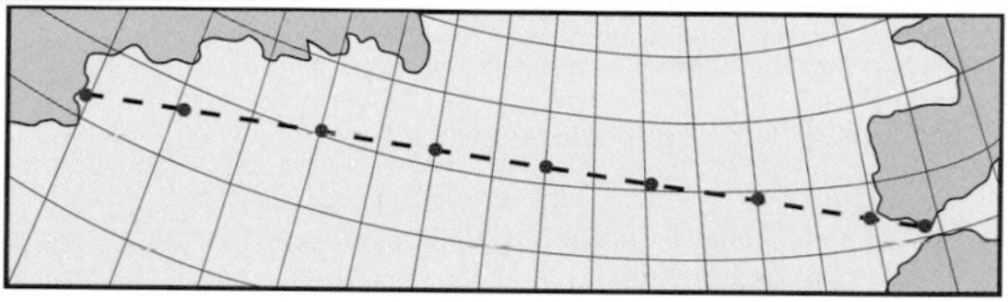

Fig 5

However, unless a boat sailing a Great Circle route is sailing directly along a meridian or round the Equator, it would cross each meridian at a different angle and its heading would have to be altered frequently to maintain a perfect Great Circle course. A more practical way of steering this course is to transfer a series of co-ordinates taken along the Great Circle track to a Mercator chart and link them to form a series of rhumb lines that closely mimic the Great Circle route (*Fig 6*).

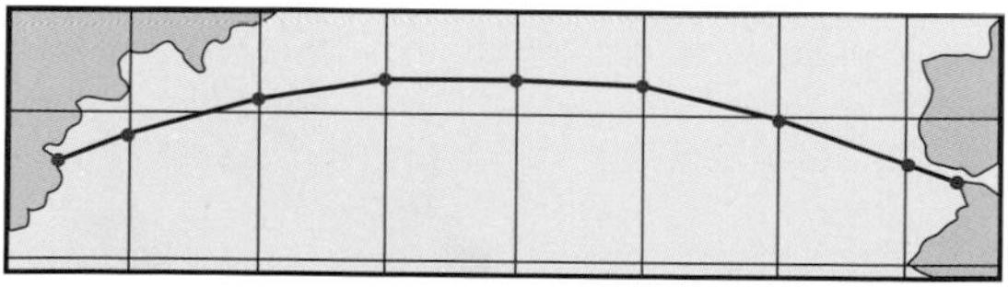

Fig 6

Measuring distance

Nautical miles

Distance at sea is measured in nautical miles, a unit based on the length of an arc that would be formed on the Earth's surface by an angle of **one minute** at the Earth's centre. The arc is measured along a meridian and therefore, one nautical mile is equivalent to one minute of latitude (*Fig 7*).

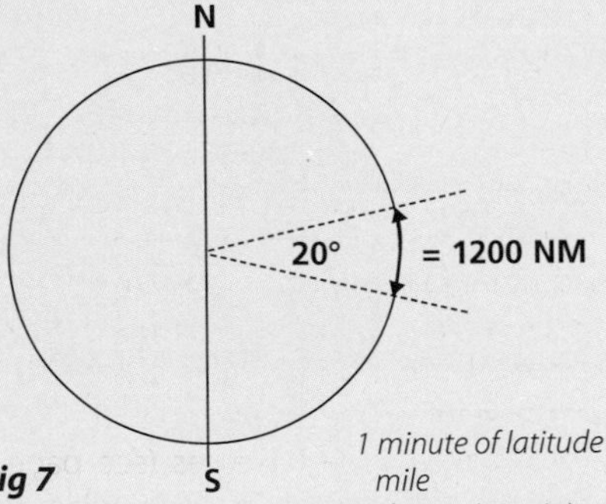

Fig 7

1 minute of latitude = 1 nautical mile
1 degree (60 min) = 60nm
10 degrees = 600nm
20 degrees = 1200nm

Because the Earth is not a perfect sphere, however, the length of one minute of latitude varies slightly, being shorter at the Equator than at the Poles and so, with international agreement, the average distance of 1852 metres (6076 feet) has been adopted as the standard length of one nautical mile.

- One degree of longitude varies from roughly 60nm at the Equator to nil at the Poles.
- The nautical mile is divisible into ten 'cables' – usually written as a decimal eg:
  5 miles and 6 cables – 5.6 miles.
- The nautical unit of speed is the 'knot', which is equivalent to one nautical mile per hour.

Measuring distance

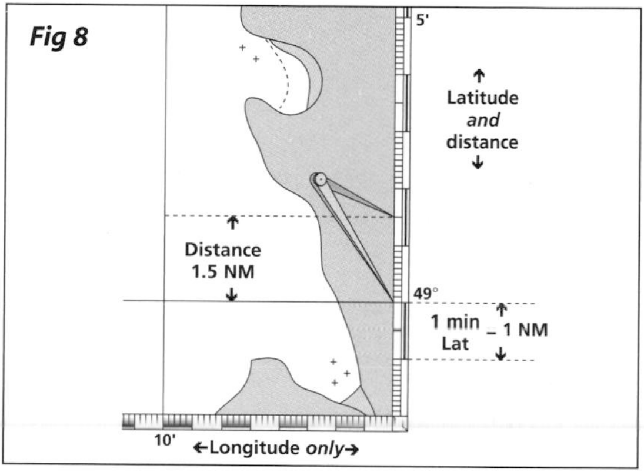

The latitude scale at the sides of a Mercator chart, where one minute of latitude is equivalent to one nautical mile, can be used to measure distance on the chart – **in any direction**. Because the latititude scale gradually changes as latitude increases (see page 2), you should only use that part of the scale adjacent to the section of the chart in use.

Caution. Never measure distance against the longitude scale (see page 6).

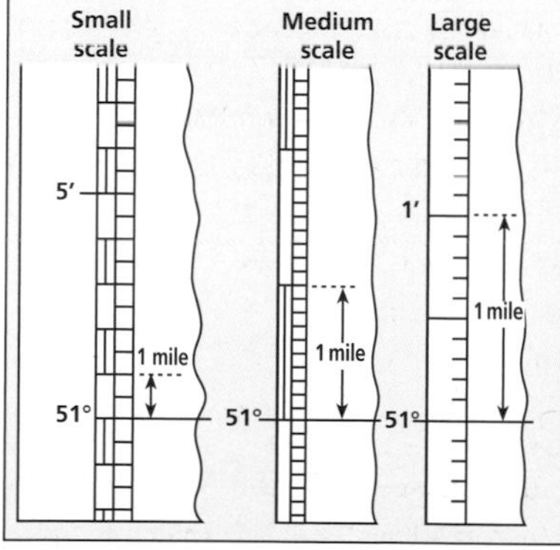

Fig 9
When changing to a different chart, be aware that the significance of the graduations changes with the chart's natural scale.

Plotting position

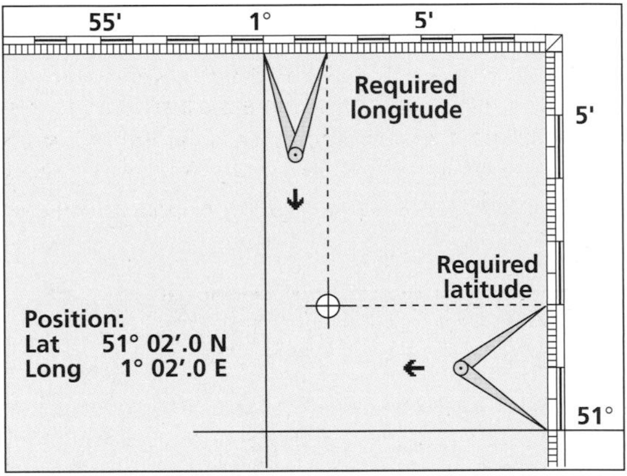

Fig 10 ***Position on the Earth's surface is expressed in terms of latitude and longitude.***

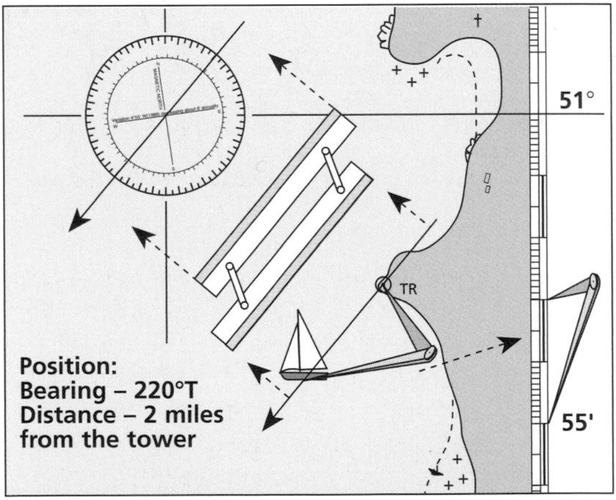

Fig 11 ***In coastal navigation, the position of a vessel is more often identified by its bearing and distance from a charted place or feature.***

Plotting position

The Breton plotter

Chart plotters are used to measure angles and plot bearings on a chart. One of the easiest plotters to use on a small boat with limited space is the 'Breton' which has only two parts: a transparent rectangular base plate surmounted with a freely rotating circular protractor (*Fig 12*).

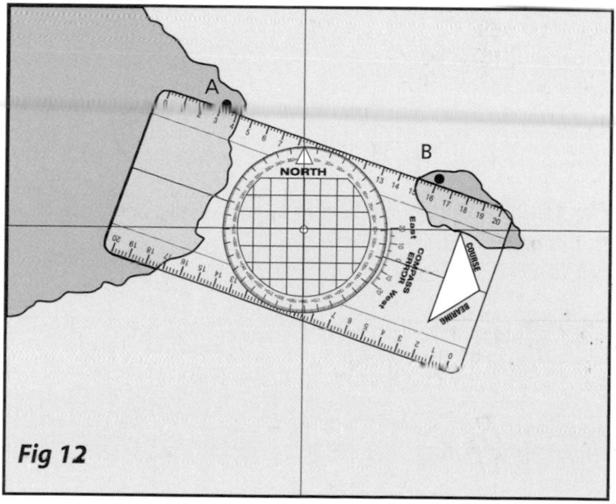

Fig 12

To use this plotter to measure the bearing of one known mark from another, align one edge, or the centreline of the base plate with both marks **A** and **B** as shown above. Then while holding this alignment firmly, turn the protractor until its grid is aligned (north to the top of the chart) with either a meridian or a parallel. Read the bearing on the protractor against the centreline of the base plate – making an allowance for magnetic variation if necessary.

Plotting position

To draw a course line, or tidal stream vector, on the chart, set the protractor to the required course or tidal stream direction. Keep the protractor setting fixed and place one edge of the base plate on either a known position or the very end of a previously drawn course line or vector **C**. Finally, rotate the whole plotter until the protractor grid – (with north pointing to the top of the chart) comes into line with either a meridian or a parallel and draw the course line or vector as required (*Fig 13*).

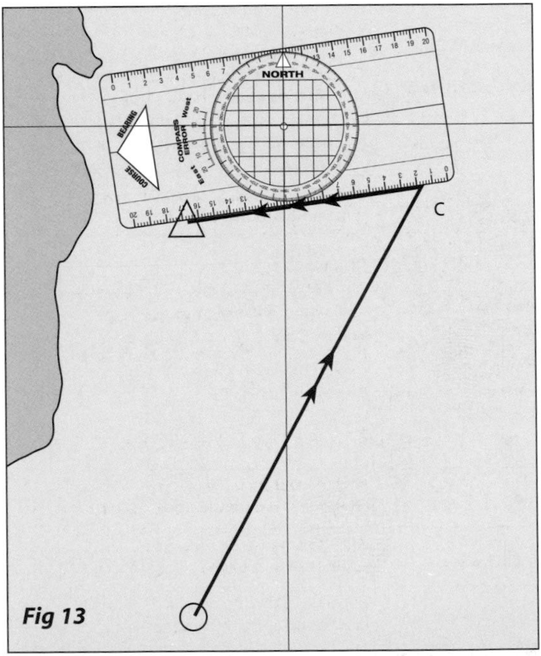

Fig 13

▸▸ Note

The arrow on the base plate should point in the direction you are **either** looking or steering.

Chart symbols

Reading the chart

On nautical charts, symbols and abbreviations are used to convey a mass of navigational information to the mariner. Each symbol has only one meaning, but it is vital that these 'coded messages' are correctly interpreted as many of them warn of specific dangers to navigation such as these:

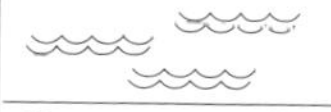	**Overfalls, tide rips, races**
	**Eddies**
	**Obstruction or danger, exact nature not specified or determined, depth unknown**
	**Obstruction, depth known**
	**Obstruction which has been swept by wire to the depth shown**
	**Breakers**
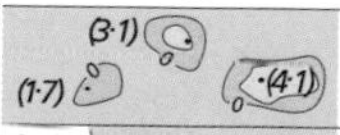	**Rock which does not cover, height above high water**
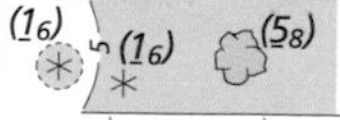	**Rock which covers and uncovers, height above chart datum**
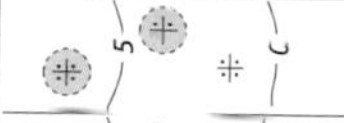	**Rock awash at the level of chart datum**
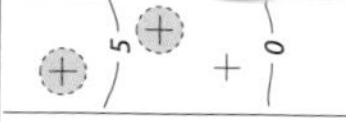	**Underwater rock, depth unknown, considered dangerous to surface navigation**
	**Wreck showing any part of hull or superstructure at the level of chart datum**
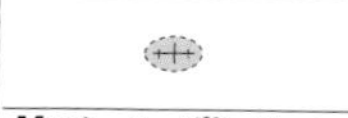	**Wreck, depth unknown which is considered dangerous to surface navigation**
	**Wreck of which the mast(s) only are visible at chart datum**

***A complete list of symbols and abbreviations is provided in the Admiralty publication,* Chart 5011.**

Chart correction

Corrections to charts

Out of date charts are potentially dangerous. Chart agents will correct them for a small fee, but with care, you can do the job yourself, using just a fine pen and the usual chart instruments.

Charts that need updating are listed in *Weekly Notices to Mariners*. The notices can be obtained from any Admiralty chart agent, who will also have copies of *Chart 5011 – Chart Symbols and Abbreviations*, which you may find useful. The notices explain the changes that need to be made to each affected chart, which, in most cases, necessitates the insertion, movement or deletion of a symbol at some specific position on the chart. Anyone who uses UKHO charts can also keep them up to date by using the Notices to Mariners Website at www.nmwebsearch.gov.uk or www.ukho.gov.uk and you can also find instructions on how to update your charts on the RYA website at www.rya.org.uk.

When making a correction, ensure that it is being made in the right place – mistakes can have serious consequences – and do not use black ink to make a correction as it may not be immediately obvious to the chart user. By convention, magenta ink should be used, but in practice any waterproof red ink will do. Where possible, a new symbol should be inserted directly onto the given position, but if the area is too cluttered, 'arrow' the new symbol in from a nearby clear space to a position dot (*Fig 14*).

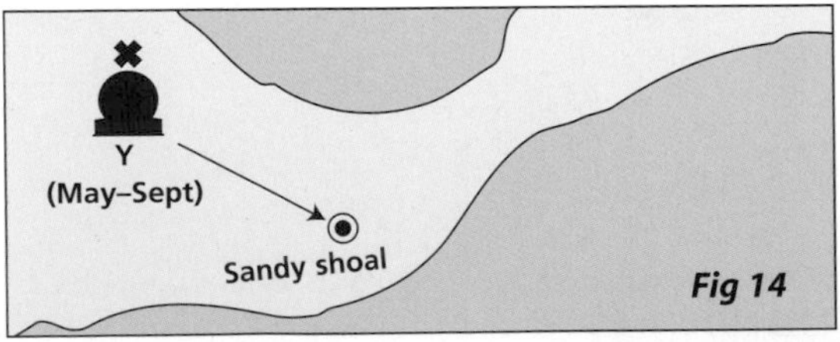

Fig 14

Chart correction

Never insert new symbols on top of existing ones (*Fig 16*). It may be possible to cover a symbol that is to be replaced by using a Tippex pen before inserting the new feature, but it is more usual to delete a symbol by drawing two straight lines through it and arrowing the replacement in to a position dot (*Fig 15*).

Fig 16

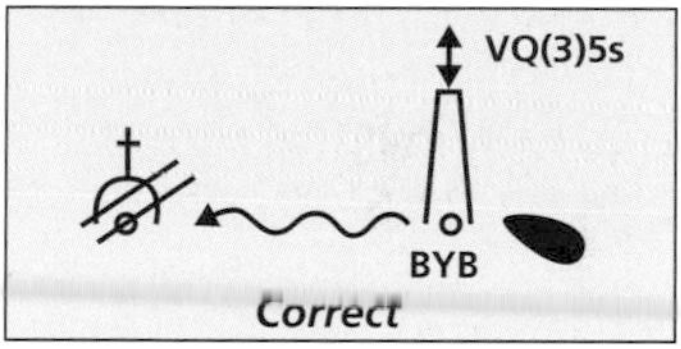

Fig 15

Short distance movement of buoys etc can be shown by arrowing them to the new position, otherwise delete them and re-insert them in the new position (*Fig 17*).

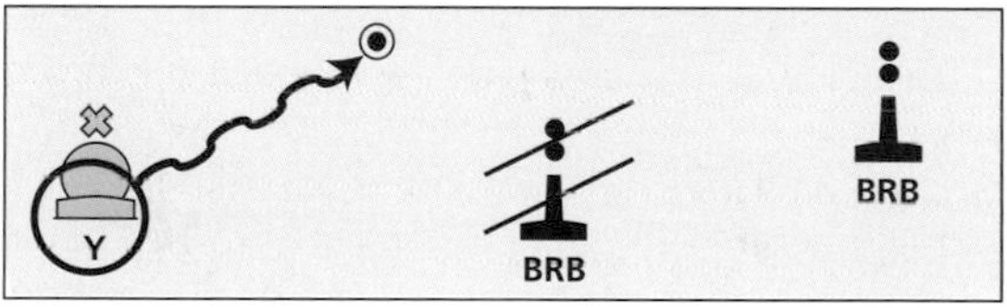

Fig 17

Major or complicated amendments are sometimes effected by using 'block' corrections. These are sections of the chart reprinted in the Notice, which must be cut out and carefully pasted into place on the chart using an adhesive such as Pritt Stick. After correcting your chart, make a note of the year and Notice number in the bottom left margin and check that the current correction is sequential to the last correction listed in the Notice.

Notices to Mariners are intended for correction to Admiralty charts but the information is also valid for Stanfords and Imray charts – and pilot books of course.

Variation

Applying variation

Direction on Earth is measured clockwise from north using 360° notation. Charts are oriented to true north but the magnetic compass used to determine direction at sea points to magnetic north. The angular difference between the direction of true and magnetic north from any given position is called variation and may be either easterly or westerly depending upon the vessel's geographic position (*Fig 1*).

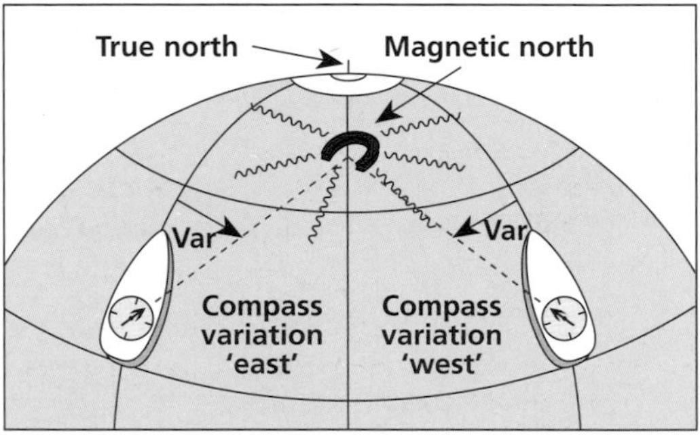

Fig 1 A magnetic compass points towards magnetic north* not *true north. Variation is the angular difference between them.

Variation not only differs from place to place but also from year to year. Local variation at the date a chart is published, together with the annual rate of change is printed on the magnetic north arrow of the compass rose, ie 4° 30′ W 2004 (9′ E).

This tells you that magnetic variation is 4° 30′ W in the year 2004 and the annual change is 9′ E (decreasing) which means that if this chart is used in the year 2008, local variation then will be 3° 54′ W – or more properly 4° 00′W, since it is usual to express variation to the nearest full degree.

Applying deviation

The magnetic compass can be affected by nearby electrical equipment or ferrous masses that deflect the compass card away from magnetic north. This effect is called deviation and may be easterly or westerly depending upon the **vessel's heading**.

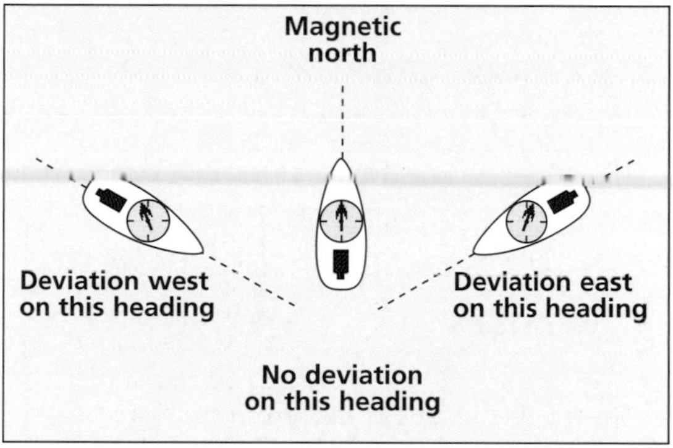

***Fig 2** The mass of this boat's engine is influencing the compass card. Each time the course is altered, the relative positions of the engine and the compass change and so does the value of deviation on that heading.*

- The difference between a compass course or bearing and a true course or bearing is the sum of variation and deviation.
- The navigator must convert the course he has steered by compass into a true course in order to plot it on the chart and conversely, he must convert a true course measured on the chart into a course he can steer by compass (see pages 18 and 19).

Checking the compass

Compass siting and checking

Compass deviation is not a problem provided that the error for each heading is known and is allowed for.

Steering compasses should be positioned where they can easily be seen by the helmsman, but as far away as possible from the influence of ferrous masses and electrical equipment. After siting, every steering compass should be checked by a qualified compass adjuster who will adjust it and then prepare a deviation card for any residual error. A typical card (*Fig 3*) shows the deviation for each of 16 headings around the compass.

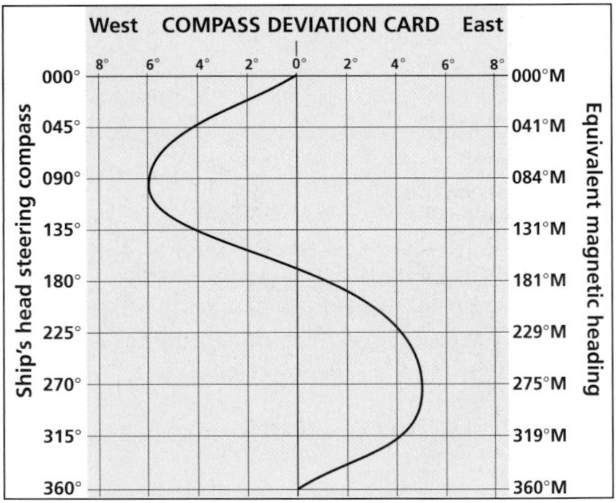

Fig 3

▶▶ Note

Deviation is measured for a given boat's heading – not for a magnetic course. Each deviation value has been applied to the boat's heading by compass to give the equivalent magnetic heading (see pages 18 and 19).

Checking the compass

It is utterly reckless to rely upon an uncorrected compass, so if for any reason its deviation is doubtful or unknown, you should run your own check on it.

A rough but reliable guide to the deviation on a single course can be obtained if you stand in the stern – well away from any magnetic influences – and sight through the mast and bow with a hand bearing compass (*Fig 4*). Compare the reading obtained with that shown by the steering compass and any difference will be the deviation on that heading.

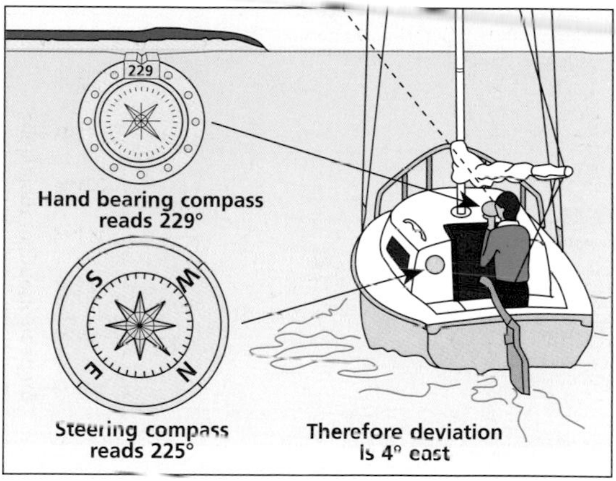

Fig 4

- If the steering compass reads ***higher*** than the hand bearing compass, deviation is ***westerly***.
- If the steering compass reads ***lower*** than the hand bearing compass, deviation is ***easterly***.
- By repeating this procedure for each of the headings shown on the card in Fig 3, you can produce your own deviation card for the steering compass in use.

Compass conversion

True bearing to compass bearing

To convert a TRUE course into a COMPASS course apply correction for variation and deviation in the sequence shown.

If the error is:

West – ***add*** the angle
East – ***subtract*** the angle

True°	Var	Mag°	Dev	Comp°
	ORDER OF WORK			

→ **W+**
E–

1 Apply variation to the ***true*** course to obtain the ***magnetic*** course.

2 Apply deviation to the ***magnetic*** course to obtain the ***compass*** course.

The appropriate variation is obtained from the chart in use.

Deviation is taken from the deviation card belonging to the steering compass being used (see pages 15 and 16).

Compass bearing to true bearing

To convert a COMPASS course into a TRUE course apply correction for deviation and variation in the sequence shown.

If the error is:

East – ***add*** the angle
West – ***subtract*** the angle

Comp°	Dev	Mag°	Var	True°
	ORDER OF WORK			

→ E+ W–

1 Apply deviation to the ***compass*** course to obtain the ***magnetic*** course.

2 Apply variation to the ***magnetic*** course to obtain the ***true*** course.

Remember – hand bearing compasses that are used in locations away from ferrous metal and electrical fields are deemed to be free of deviation and therefore bearings taken with them are 'magnetic' and only need to be corrected for variation to convert them to true.

✱ Top tip

The word 'CADET' can be a useful reminder that to go from Compass to True you need to Add Easterly variation and deviation ie:

C° AD E T°

Cause of leeway

What is leeway?

Leeway is the angle between the direction of the boat's heading and the direction in which she is actually moving through the water as a result of being blown sideways (off course) by the wind.

The amount of leeway experienced depends largely upon the strength of the wind and the speed at which the boat is moving. It varies from boat to boat depending upon the hull design, draught, 'windage' of the superstructure or rigging, and, not least, upon the 'point of sailing'. Leeway is usually at its greatest when sailing close hauled – particularly if the helmsman is 'pinching', which causes excessive heeling and a reduction in the lateral resistance of the keel; it is at its least when running downwind or motoring head-to-wind.

Motor cruisers that have high topsides will often make more leeway than a sailing yacht because they lack the benefit of a deep keel to increase their lateral resistance.

In Fig 1, A–B is the boat's course (the direction in which she is pointing). If no other influence affects that course she will eventually arrive at B but, with wind on the port beam, say, the boat will be blown to leeward (downwind) of the course being steered and will in fact move along line A–D although at all times her heading has remained parallel to A–B. The line A–D is therefore the boat's track through the water and the angle that A–D makes with A–B is the 'leeway angle', for which an allowance must be made if serious errors in estimated position or shaping a course to steer is to be avoided.

With wind on the starboard beam, leeway would be in the opposite direction of course and the boat's track would then be along line A–C.

Cause of leeway

Wind from port side:
Water track is *greater* than the heading

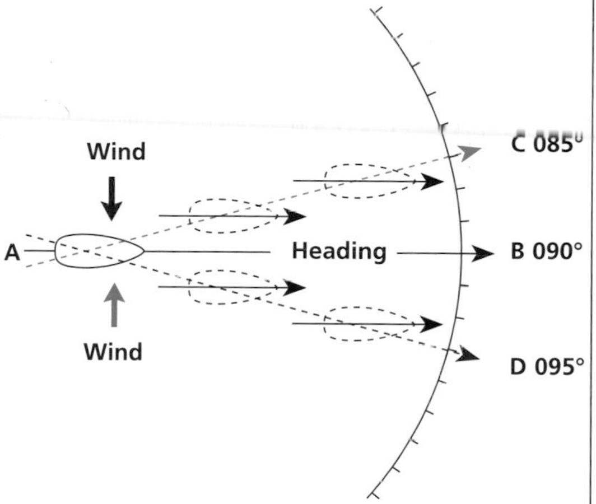

Wind from starboard side:
Water track is *less* than the heading

Fig 1

Allowing for leeway

Before you can make an allowance for leeway, its magnitude must first be measured or estimated but, because boats and conditions vary so widely, there are no sophisticated ways of doing this and the various methods that are employed are all little more than guesswork. In general though, it is reasonable to assume that the average sailboat will make between 3 and 5 degrees leeway in a 7-knot breeze and 5 to 8 degrees in a strong 20-knot wind.

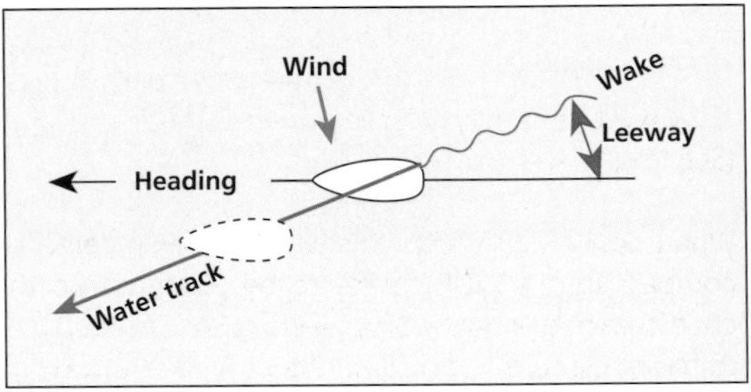

Fig 2

It is often possible to estimate leeway by using buoys or shore marks when there is little or no tidal stream, but perhaps the simplest method is to look aft and estimate the angle between the boat's fore and aft line and its wake (*Fig 2*).

Unfortunately, whilst this method produces quite reasonable results, just when leeway is likely to be at its maximum – when sailing close hauled in a lumpy sea for instance – the wake is not always very clear, and so at times like this or whenever there is doubt, always try to be upwind (and uptide) of your destination, especially when approaching the coast at right angles.

Allowing for leeway

Having estimated the boat's leeway by whatever means, due allowance can now be made by either adding or subtracting the appropriate leeway angle to or from the boat's heading before you draw the course on the chart, ie:

When converting a TRUE course taken from the chart into a course to steer by compass, make an allowance for leeway that is anticipated by applying the appropriate angle to WINDWARD of the TRUE course as follows:

Wind from port – *subtract* the angle
Wind from starboard – *add* the angle

(See Course to steer page 39.)

When converting a course that has been steered by compass into a TRUE course to be plotted onto the chart, make an allowance for leeway which is estimated to have occurred by applying the appropriate angle to LEEWARD (downwind) of the TRUE course steered as follows:

Wind from port – *add* the angle
Wind from starboard – *subtract* the angle.

(See Estimating position page 48.)

✷ Top tip

An arrow drawn on the chart to indicate wind direction will help you to visualise the wind relative to the boat's heading and ensure that any allowance for leeway is applied in the right direction.

Tides

'Tides' are the vertical rise and fall of the sea's surface caused by the gravitational pull of the Sun and Moon. When the Sun and Moon are in line with the Earth, their combined influence creates very high and very low waters known as **spring** tides, but when the Sun and Moon are at right angles to the Earth, their effect is much less and so more moderate **neap** tides occur (*Fig 1*).

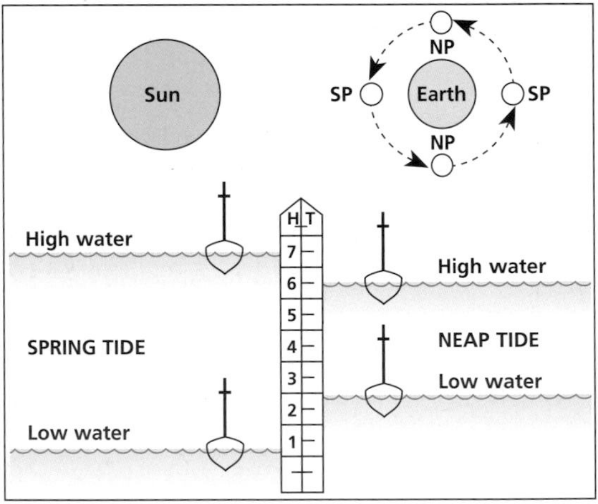

Fig 1

Spring tides occur about every 14 days at the time of full and new Moons. Neap tides occur during the alternate weeks when the Moon is in its first or third quarter (*Fig 2*).

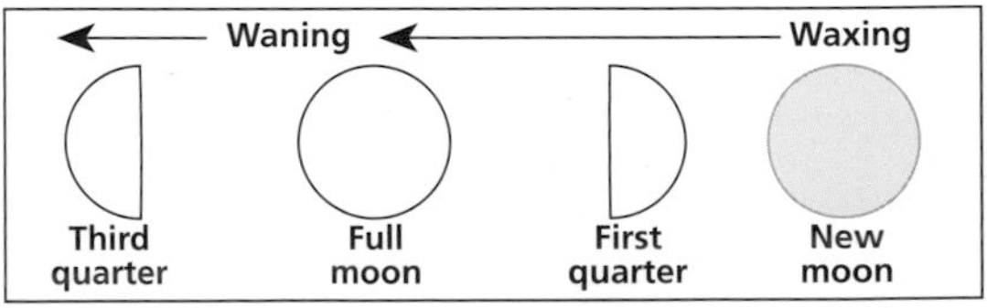

Fig 2

Tidal patterns

The rise and fall of sea level is caused by the gravitational forces of the moon and the sun but they only become noticeable in shallower inshore waters. Many factors such as the depth of the water, or the size and shape of the coast affect the tide, and no two places have exactly the same tidal pattern. Some places such as the Severn estuary (Britain), Darwin (Australia) and the Bay of Fundy (Canada) have exceptionally high tides, while others like the Baltic and Mediterranean seas have little or no tide at all.

Around the British Isles, north western Europe and most of the east coast of North America, tides are *semi-diurnal* (twice daily), having two high tides of more or less the same height and two low tides also of roughly equal heights with an interval of approximately 12 hours 25 minutes between successive high waters (*Fig 3*).

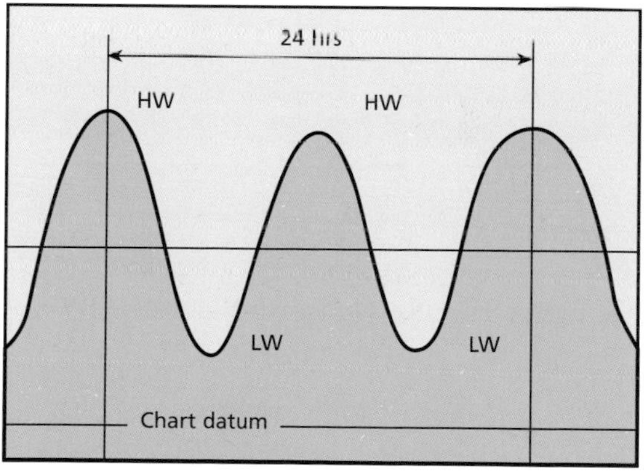

Fig 3 Semi-diurnal tide.

Tidal patterns

Tides around Australia, the Pacific in general, and along the northern Gulf of Mexico are mostly *diurnal* (once daily) and have only one high and one low water each tidal day. The height of successive high or low waters does not vary greatly (*Fig 4*).

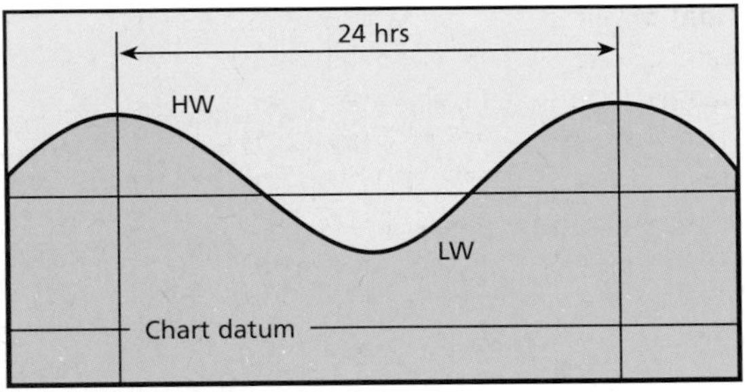

Fig 4 Diurnal tide.

The Pacific coast of North America experiences tides known as *mixed tides*. These have two high and two low waters each day but, unlike other semi-diurnal tides, the first and second tides of each day vary considerably in height (*Fig 5*).

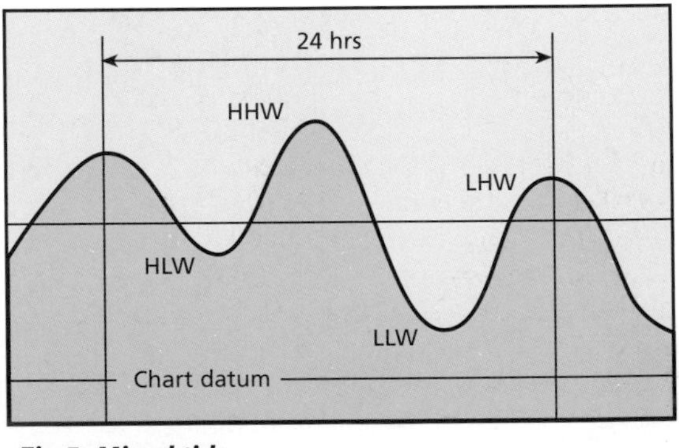

Fig 5 Mixed tide.

Height of tide Times and heights of all high and low waters for each day of the year are given in tide tables and nautical almanacs together with instructions for calculating the height of tide at any given time between high and low water.

Tidal streams are the horizontal movement of the water caused by the rise and fall of the tide. Spring tides create strong streams, and neap tides relatively weaker ones. The direction and strength of tidal stream in an area is shown on charts and in tidal atlases and is directly related to the time of high water and the **range of tide** at a specific standard port. The range of tide is the vertical difference in height between successive low and high waters (see *Fig 6* and page 28).

Fig 6

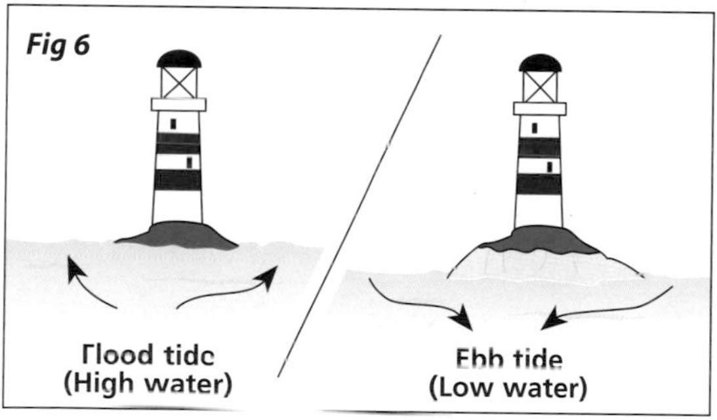

The incoming tide is called **the flood** and the outgoing tide, **the ebb** which, in most locations, is stronger and lasts longer than the flood.

At high and low tide, the water stops rising or falling for a short period of time known as the '**stand of the tide**'.

The 'interval' between successive high waters around the British Isles is approximately 12 hr 25 min.

Definition of tidal levels

The level of the sea is constantly changing as the tide rises and falls and so, on a chart, depths of water and drying heights are measured from a common state of the tide known as the Lowest Astronomical Tide (LAT). This is the lowest level to which the tide is expected to fall due to any combination of astronomical conditions and is the **chart datum**.

Chart datum The level to which soundings and drying heights are referred on the chart and the level above which height of tide is measured.

Charted sounding The depth to the sea bed below the level of chart datum. Shown on the chart by figures in metres and tenths of metres, eg 6_5

Drying height The height above chart datum of a feature that is periodically covered and uncovered by the tide shown on the chart by *underlined* figures in metres and tenths of metres, eg $\underline{2}_4$

Height of tide The vertical distance between chart datum and the sea level at any given time.

Mean High Water Springs (MHWS) and **Mean Low Water Springs (MLWS)** The average height of high and low water at spring tides.

Mean High Water Neaps (MHWN) and **Mean Low Water Neaps (MLWN)** The average height of high and low water at neap tides.

MHWS is the level from which the elevation of a charted terrestrial object is measured.

Highest Astronomical Tide (HAT) The highest sea level likely to occur due to any combination of meteorological or astronomical conditions. In areas with an appreciable tidal range, vertical clearance under bridges, overhead pipes and cables is measured above the level of HAT. Elsewhere, tidal range clearance will continue to be measured above MHWS or MHW levels. *(See note below chart title for relevant clearance datum.)*

Tidal definitions

Tidal heights and chart datum

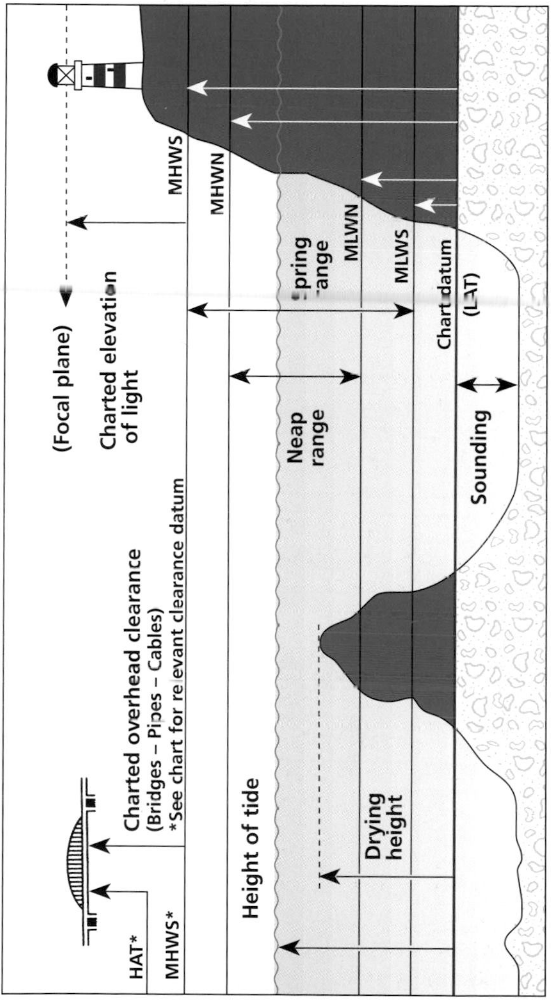

Effect of tidal streams

All vessels afloat in tidal waters are affected by tidal streams – the horizontal movement of the sea caused by the rise and fall of the tide. The direction in which the stream is moving is called the **set**; the speed at which it moves is the **rate**; and the distance the stream (and everything afloat in it) travels in a given time is called the **drift**, for example:

SET 090°, RATE 2 knots = an eastward DRIFT of 2 nautical miles in one hour (Fig 7).

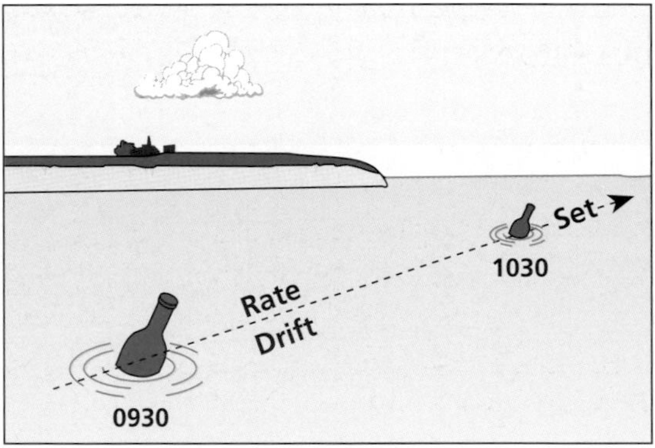

Fig 7

The set of the tidal stream relative to the boat's heading may assist progress (*Fig 8*) or hinder it (*Fig 9*) but it may also push you off course (*Fig 10*); in which case you will have to compensate for 'lateral drift' by steering up into the stream slightly and 'crabbing' along the desired course. The precise angle at which you need to steer the boat is determined by the speed of the boat through the water and by the rate and set of the tidal stream (see Course to steer page 39).

Effect of tidal streams

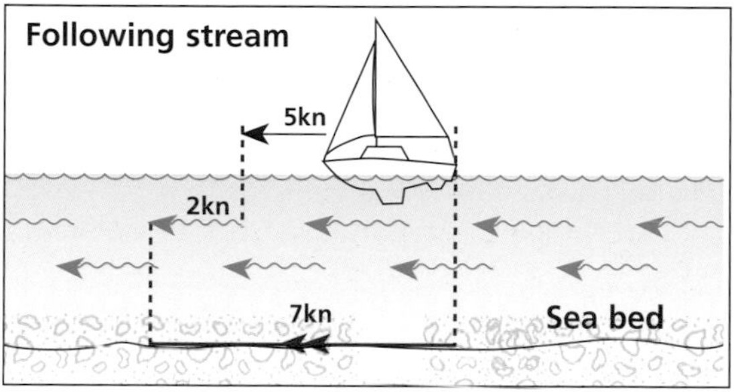

Fig 8 Speed over ground = boat speed plus tidal stream.

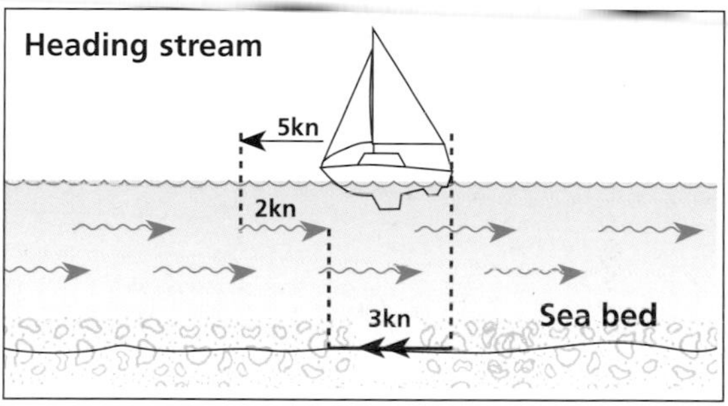

Fig 9 Speed over ground = boat speed minus tidal stream.

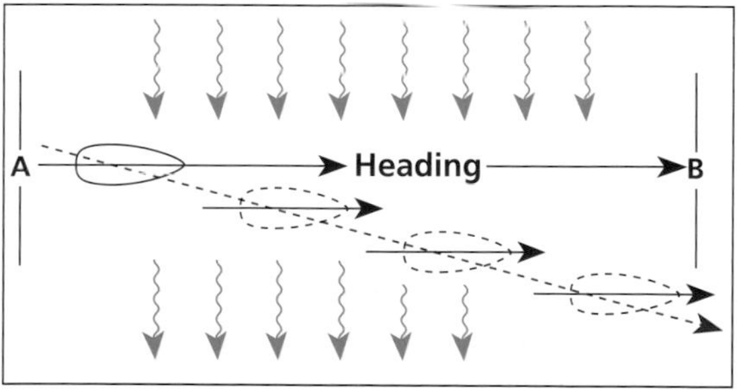

Fig 10 Tidal stream setting vessel off course to starboard.

Tidal stream information

Sources of information

Information concerning tidal streams can be found on Admiralty charts and in tidal atlases.

Admiralty charts Positions where tidal streams have been measured are marked on Admiralty charts by a letter within a diamond. An associated table shows the set and the spring and neap rate of the streams at these positions for each hour before and after HW at the standard port (*Fig 11*).

Tidal atlases have a separate page for each hour before and after HW at a standard port upon which the set of the tidal stream is depicted by arrows with figures alongside to indicate the mean rate in tenths of a knot. The first pair of numbers show the rate at neaps and the second pair, the rate at springs (*Fig 12*).

To use either method you must first obtain the time of HW at the relevant standard port and pencil it in on chart or atlas together with the times +/– HW as required. You can then see at a glance what the tide is doing at any particular time.

Reeds Nautical Almanac and the excellent **tidal atlases** produced by the late Michael Reeve-Fowkes also provide the same information in different forms and both include full instructions for their use.

Tide tables for specific Standard Ports are published annually and show the times and heights of high and low water on a daily basis throughout the year.

Nautical almanacs comprise a selection of tide tables for the area covered, together with information enabling tidal predictions to be made for those smaller Secondary Ports for which tide tables are not usually provided (see page 72).

Fig 11 Tidal stream tables (top) and a chart extract (below) showing tidal diamond B.

Tidal Streams referred to HW Dover

		A 50°42'3N 0 26'5E		B 50°53'0N 1 00'6E			C 51°01'0N 1 10'0E			D 51°09'7N 1 27'8E			D 51°03'0N 1 40'0E		
			Rate *(kn)*			Rate *(kn)*			Rate *(kn)*			Rate *(kn)*			Rate *(kn)*	
Hours	Dir	Sp	Np	Dir	Sp	Np	Dir	Sp	Np	Dir	Sp	Np	Dir	Sp	Np	
Before HW 6	248	0.8	0.4	211	1.6	0.9	224	0.9	0.5	212	2.2	1.2	220	1.7	0.9	
Before HW 5	067	0.5	0.3	211	2.1	1.2	239	1.0	0.6	213	2.2	1.2	220	2.8	1.6	
Before HW 4	068	1.9	1.0	211	1.8	1.1	235	1.1	0.6	216	1.9	1.1	220	3.5	2.0	
Before HW 3	068	2.6	1.5	211	0.9	0.5	242	0.6	0.4	228	1.3	0.8	220	2.8	1.6	
Before HW 2	068	2.3	1.3	*Slack*			*Slack*			*Slack*			220	1.2	0.7	
Before HW 1	068	1.2	0.6	031	0.8	0.5	052	0.6	0.3	032	1.2	1.7	040	0.8	0.4	
HW	067	0.1	0.1	031	1.5	0.8	049	1.2	0.7	038	2.0	1.2	040	2.5	0.1	
After HW 1	248	0.9	0.5	031	1.9	1.1	049	1.3	0.7	039	2.3	1.3	040	3.4	1.9	
After HW 2	247	1.4	0.8	031	1.7	1.0	156	1.0	0.5	034	2.2	1.2	040	2.9	1.6	

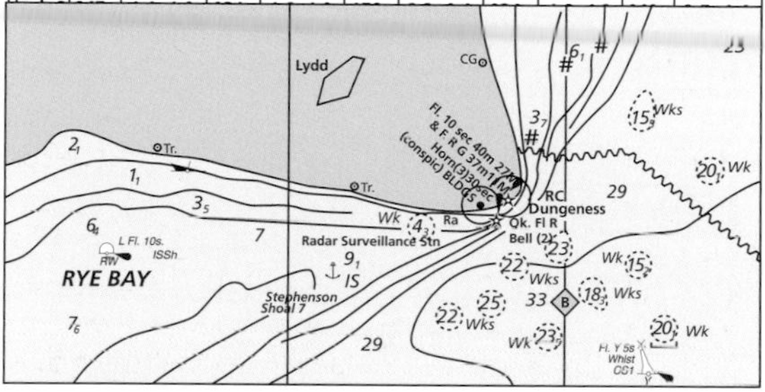

Fig 12 Tidal atlas chartlets.

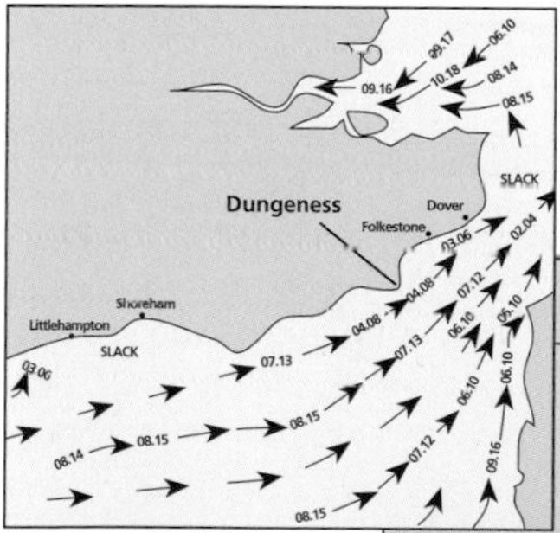

1 hour before HW Dover

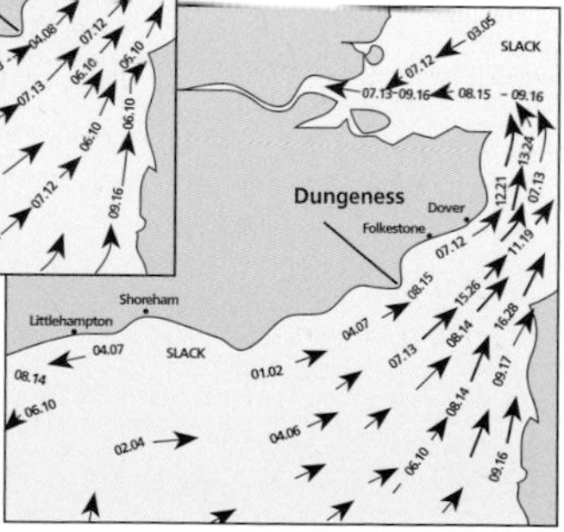

HW Dover

Tidal streams – interpolation

Interpolation of rate

The rate of tidal streams is assumed to vary with the range of tide at the standard port. For times **between** full springs and neaps you must interpolate between the rates given in order to plot accurate tidal vectors when estimating position or finding a course to steer. This can be done by using the Computation of Rate Graph supplied with the atlas (*Fig 14* opposite), or arithmetically with the formula:

$$\frac{\textbf{Range of tide for day}}{\textbf{Spring range of tide}} \times \textbf{Spring rate of tidal stream}$$

Remember that if your course passes through an area marked by more than one tidal diamond or falls between two tidal stream arrows, it is also necessary to estimate what the rate is likely to be in the area between these positions (*Fig 13*).

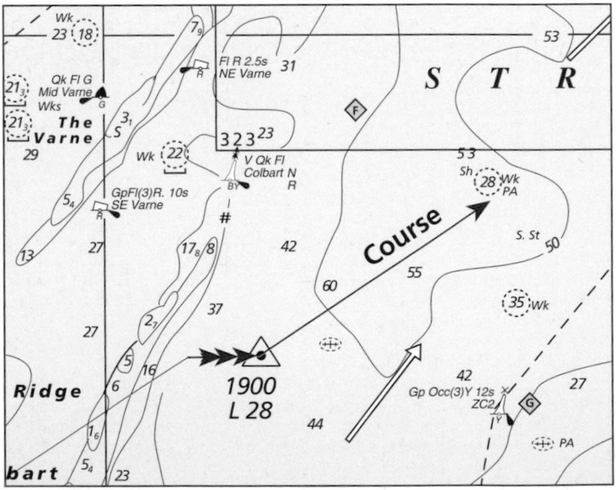

Fig 13

Tidal streams – interpolation

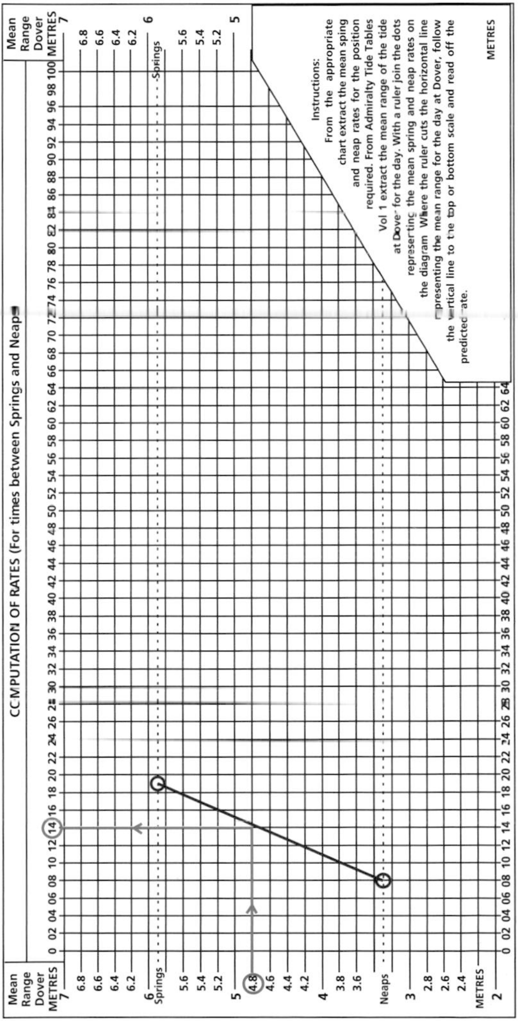

***Fig 14** An example: Range of tide from tide tables: 4.8m. Spring and neap rates of stream from chart 1.9–0.8kn. Mean rate from graph 1.4kn.*

Coastal tidal streams

Tidal streams along the coast

In many places around the coasts of Britain and northern Europe, tidal streams are strong enough to markedly affect the progress of sailing yachts and displacement motor cruisers especially when they are going to windward. It makes sense, therefore, to plan your passage so as to take advantage of favourable tidal streams and to minimize the effect of contrary ones, keeping in mind that close inshore, streams can be quite different to those predicted for an area in general.

The strength and speed of tidal streams inshore is determined to a large extent by the geography of the area. Irregularities of the coastline and obstructions to the flow caused by ridges or shoals on the sea bed combine to affect the pattern of behaviour of the streams and sometimes give rise to races, overfalls, and tide rips (*Fig 15*).

Headlands Tidal streams running parallel to the coast will run more strongly past headlands (**A**) and less so within bays into which they have a tendency to set, sometimes with a 'counter current' or back eddy developing in the tidal lee of the headland (**B**).

Channels A tidal stream which is obliged to flow through a narrow channel or converge with a stream from a different direction may speed up to form a race against which, passage is virtually impossible, and during bad weather, these areas are best avoided altogether (**C**).

Overfalls A ledge or steep-faced shoal on the sea bed may deflect a tidal stream upwards causing broken water or 'overfalls' on the surface which, in strong wind-over-tide situations, can be very dangerous (**D**).

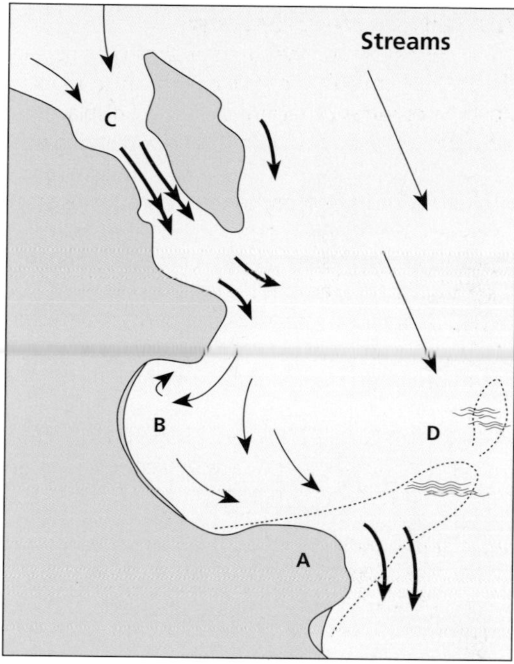

Fig 15

Sea state Strong winds and tidal streams can have a marked effect on the 'sea state'. When the wind and tidal stream are in roughly the same direction, waves will be lower and longer than the wind strength might suggest but when the stream turns to flow against the wind direction the waves become higher and steeper with the likelihood of breaking crests. Fast motorboats need to slow down in wind over tide conditions and so it might be worthwhile to plan a passage against both wind and tide to take advantage of higher speeds that are possible in relatively smoother seas.

Course to steer – short period

1. On the chart (*Fig 1*), plot the required ground track from start to finish: **A–B**.

2. From the starting point, plot the set of the tidal stream that will affect the boat's course, using units of length equal to its rate in knots: **A–C**.

3. With dividers centred at the end of the tidal stream line (**C**) and set to a radius equal to the anticipated speed of the boat through the water, swing an arc to cut the ground track (**D**).

   This cut may go beyond, or fall short of **B** depending on the speed of the boat and the set and rate of the tidal stream affecting the course.

4. A line drawn between the end of the tidal stream line and the cut at (**D**) is the required water track: **C–D**.

5. Measure the TRUE bearing of the water track and to **windward** of it make an allowance to offset any leeway expected. This is now the course to steer TRUE: **C–E**.

6. Apply variation and deviation to this course as necessary to obtain the course to steer by compass (see page 18).

▸▸ Note

Vector triangles are usually drawn for periods of one hour, although longer or shorter periods may be used if appropriate. Whichever timescale is chosen, it is essential to use the same ratio for each vector ie one hour of tidal drift with one hour of boat speed.

Course to steer – short period

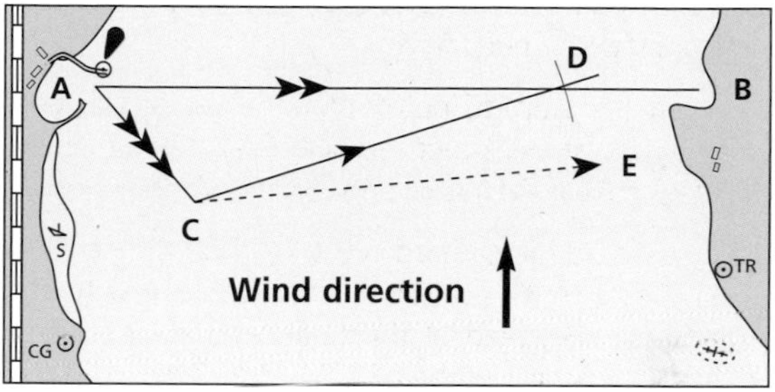

Fig 1

Leeway allowance

This is applied to the required water track:

- Wind from **port** side – **subtract** the angle
- Wind from **starboard** side – **add** the angle

Compass conversion

This is applied to the course to steer TRUE:

- Variation/deviation **east** – **subtract** the error
- Variation/deviation **west** – **add** the error

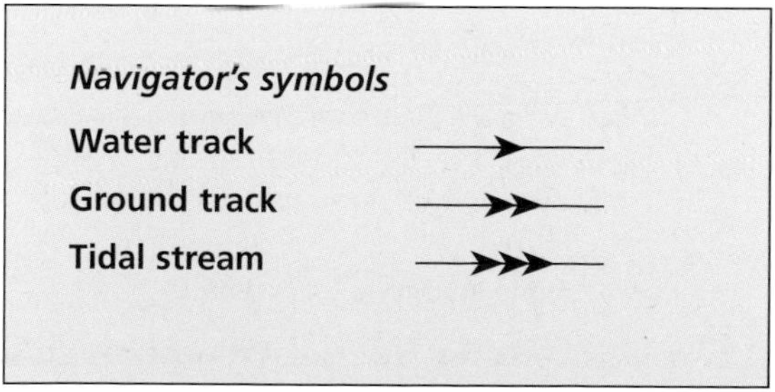

Tidal streams – longer passages

Tidal streams usually take one of two main forms:

Rectilinear, where they flow in one direction for half a tide and then reverse to flow in the opposite direction with a period of slack water at the turn of the tide *or:* **Rotary**, in which the stream changes direction from hour to hour, often without a period of slack water.

To find the course to steer across a channel having rectilinear streams (*Fig 2*), work out how long the passage is likely to take by measuring the distance across – in this case 60 miles. Dividing this distance by the anticipated speed of the boat, say 6 knots, suggests a 10-hour passage. This also tells you that you must make allowance for 10 hours of tidal stream during the crossing; so first establish what the set and rate of tidal stream will be at the time you intend to set off, then find out what the tide will be doing for the rest of the trip and add up all the westerly and then the easterly streams and subtract one from the other.

Finally, plot the balance of tide as a vector from the starting position (*Fig 3*) and lay off the distance to travel from the end of it. Apply leeway, variation and deviation in the usual way to obtain the course to steer.

To make a crossing with rotary streams (*Fig 4*) find the distance and crossing time as before but this time plot tidal vectors for each successive hour and link them as shown. From the end of this chain lay off the distance to travel and apply leeway, variation and deviation to obtain the course to steer.

- **Slack water** When there is little or no tidal stream at the 'turn of the tide'.
- **Stand of the tide** When the tide is no longer rising or falling.

(These two events rarely coincide.)

Rectilinear tidal streams

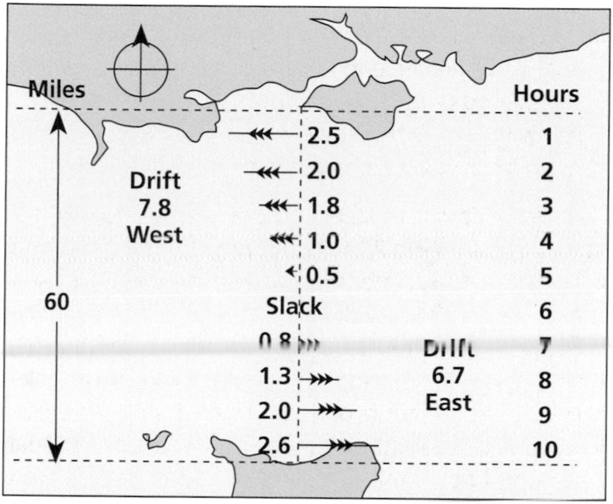

Fig 2 The movement of tidal streams for the period.

Distance to go ÷ Estimated speed = Time to cross

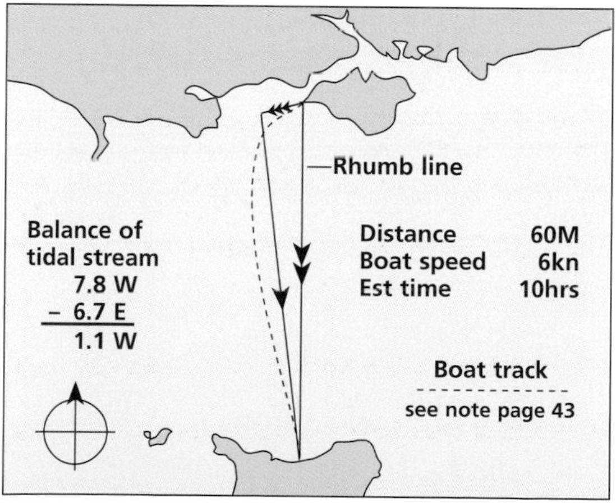

Fig 3 Plotting the balance of tide.

Course to steer – longer passages

Rotary tidal streams

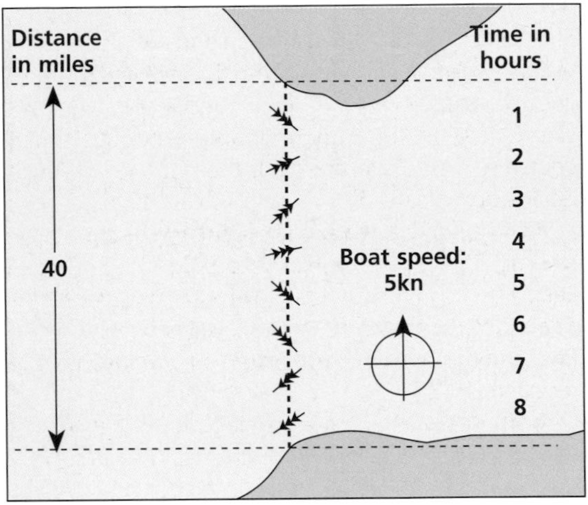

Fig 4

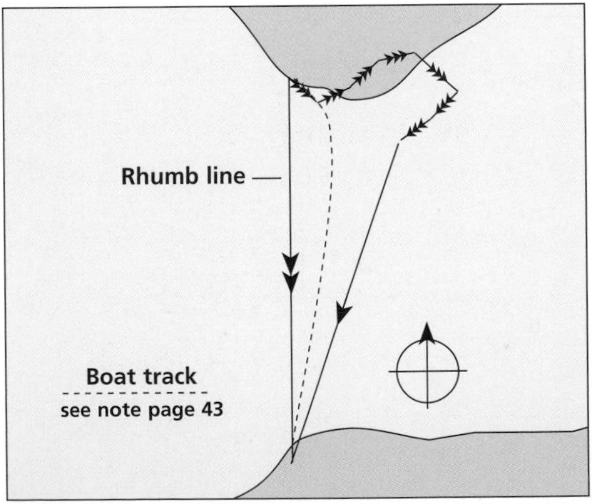

Fig 5

▶▶ Note

Steering a single course across an ebb and flood tide will take the boat well away from the required rhumb line so make certain that no dangers exist on either side. Plot an EP for every hour and work out a new course to steer each time that the distance to your destination is halved.

The alternative is to shape a separate course to steer for each hour of tidal stream (*Fig 5*). This will keep the boat on or close to the rhumb line but depending upon wind direction, a sailing vessel may find it difficult to achieve some of the headings required (*Fig 6*).

A Rhumb line is a straight line drawn between any two points on a Mercator chart and shows the true course to follow from one to the other.

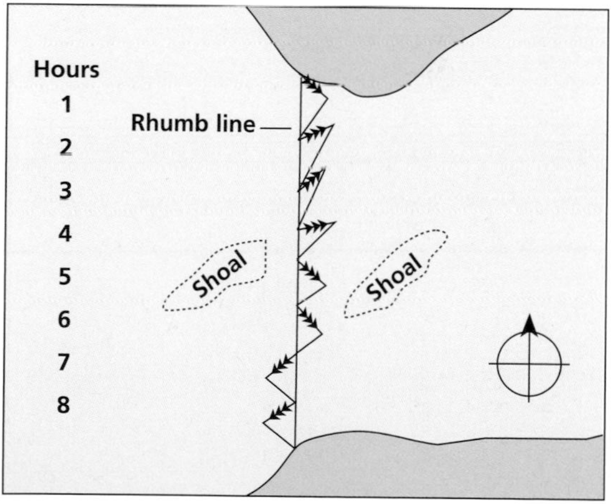

Fig 6

Sailing to windward

Destination to windward

When your destination lies directly up wind of the boat, it becomes necessary to beat towards it by sailing close-hauled on alternate tacks, preferably keeping within 10°–15° of the downwind line so as to be well placed to take advantage of any wind shifts as they occur.

Set off on the tack which points more directly toward your destination and work up to it with a series of relatively short tacks made between predetermined tack 'limiting lines', making due allowance for leeway and tidal stream in the usual way. Alternatively, if your objective is visible you can tack each time the appropriate bearing to either side of the direct line of approach is reached (*Fig 7*).

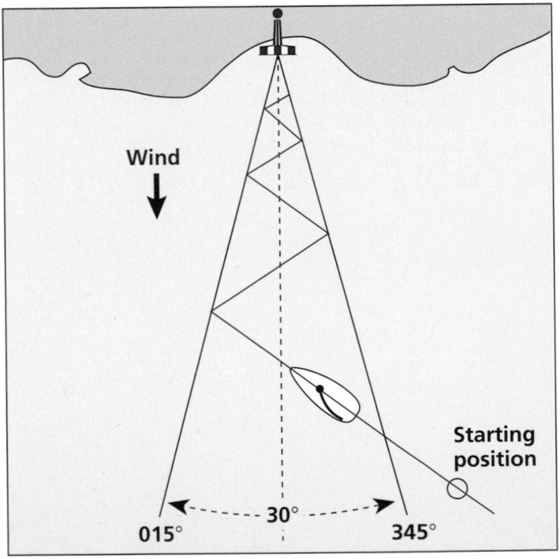

Fig 7

Lee bowing the tide

If the tidal stream is expected to slacken or reverse direction, there is an advantage to be gained from holding the tack which puts the tide on the lee bow and letting it push the boat to windward. The freeing wind shift induced by the tide will also allow the boat to point higher on this tack, helping to get you towards your destination more quickly.

If the tidal stream is constant, however, there is no advantage to 'lee bowing' as you will lose whatever you have gained when you go onto the opposite tack (*Fig 8*).

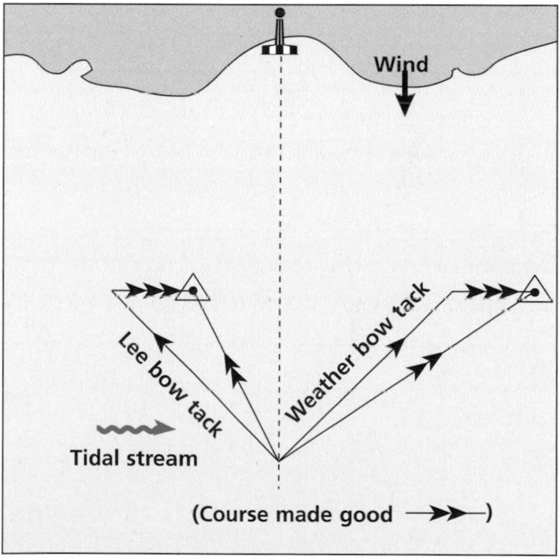

Fig 8

Sailing to windward

Laying the windward mark

When nearing your destination, and wind and tide are unlikely to change, use this method to decide when to make your final tack to lay the mark (*Fig 9*).

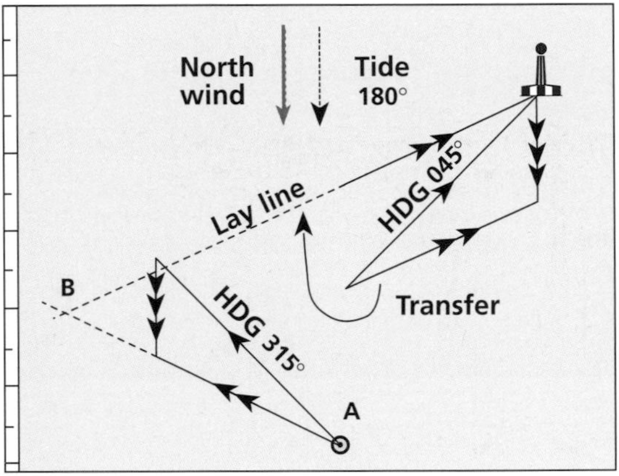

Fig 9

You are at point **A** on starboard tack, heading 315° at 4kn and your boat will tack through 90°. Tidal stream rate is 1·5kn. First, find out what the ground track will be from **A** and extend it, then work out what the ground track will be as you head for the buoy on port tack. To do this, draw the water track ***backwards*** from the buoy and mark off 4 miles for boat speed. Plot 1·5 miles of tidal stream from the buoy and connect the end of this line to the end of the water track to form the ground track. Transfer it to the buoy as shown and extend it to cut the first ground track at **B**. This is your lay line – the most leeward course you can sail to lay the buoy, and **B** is the point at which to tack. The length of the ground track shows that boat speed over the ground is about 3.1kn and since the distance to **B** from **A** is almost 4.5 miles, you should reach position **B** in about 87 minutes.

Estimated time of arrival (ETA)

To calculate ***when*** you will get there, you must know the distance to your destination, the boat's speed through the water, and what the tide is doing:

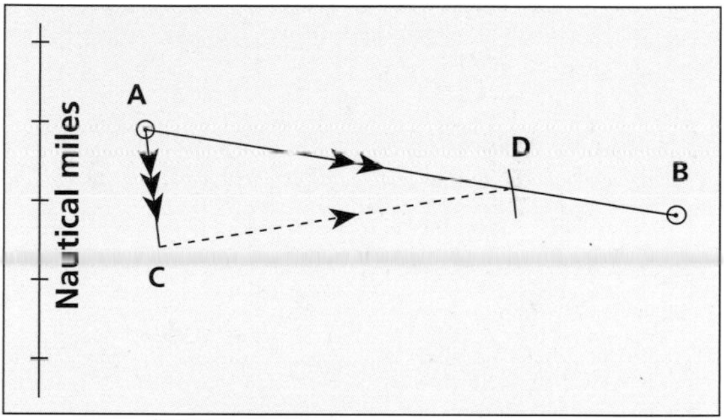

A **Starting position**

B **Destination**

A–B **Distance to go (6·9M)**

A–C **Tidal stream vector (1·5kn)**

From **C** with dividers set at a distance equal to the boat's speed through the water (4·5kn), swing an arc to cut line **A–B** at point **D**.

A–D is the speed (and distance) made good, (4·8kn) therefore **A–B x 60 ÷ A–D** is equal to the time in minutes that it will take to sail from **A** to **B** and if this time is added to your time of departure from position **A** then this will be your ETA at your destination.

$$\frac{A\text{–}B}{A\text{–}D} \times 60 = 86{\cdot}25 \text{ mins} -$$

say 1½ hrs approx.

EP – Estimated Position

Estimating your position

When making any passage at sea, an estimate of the vessel's position should be maintained at all times by carefully recording the course steered and distance run, and by allowing for all the factors that might have affected that course such as tidal stream, leeway and surface drift.

How to estimate your position (EP)

1 Convert the course steered by compass to TRUE by applying deviation and variation as appropriate **A–B** (this is not usually drawn on the chart).

2 Adjust the bearing of the course **A–B** to leeward (downwind) by the amount of leeway suffered to obtain the *water track* TRUE.

3 From the last known position on the chart plot the water track and along it mark off the distance run according to the log **A–C**.

4 From point **C** plot the set of tidal stream experienced using units of length equal to its rate in knots **C–D**.

5 Point **D** is the boat's estimated position and a line drawn between it and the last known position (**A**) is the *course made good* (or *ground track*) and the distance along it is the actual distance covered over the ground **A–D**.

This distance, divided by the elapsed time, is the boat's effective *speed over the ground*.

Plotting the estimated position (EP)

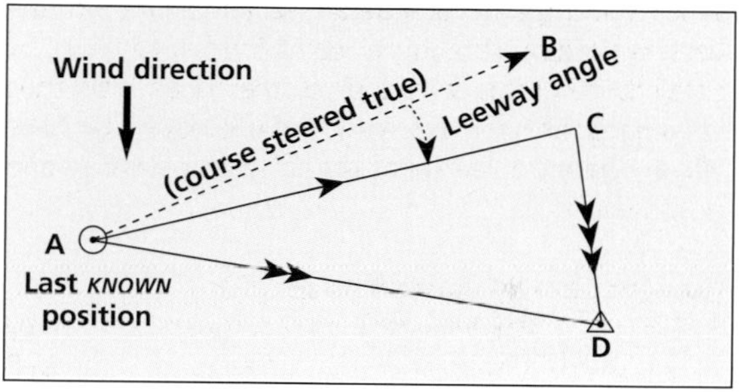

Compass conversion This is applied to the course steered by compass.

- Variation/deviation **east** – **add** the error
- Variation/deviation **west** – **subtract** the error

Estimated leeway suffered This is applied to the course steered TRUE.

- Wind from **port** side – **add** the angle
- Wind from **starboard** side – **subtract** the angle

Navigator's symbols

Water track

Ground track

Tidal stream

Fix **EP**

DR – EP

Dead reckoning and estimated position

A position derived just from the course steered and the distance the boat has travelled through the water is called a *dead reckoning* or DR position. A more accurate variant of this is where the effect of leeway has also been taken into consideration thereby showing the boat's actual *track* through the water but either way, the position so found will be nothing more than a place 'somewhere in the water'.

Estimated position

An *estimated position* is a refinement of the DR where the influence of both leeway *and* tidal stream has been reflected so as to show the boat's position relative to the sea bed. Sadly, the procedure for estimating position is far from perfect, and so errors tend to accumulate in the reckoning which means that the boat's position must periodically be 'fixed' relative to the land if the plot is not to become more and more uncertain as time passes. One 'tried and tested' method of fixing position, when coastal sailing, is that of taking visual bearings on charted objects by *hand bearing compass*.

Position lines

When the bearing of a known object is drawn onto a chart it is called a *position line* and the observer's boat *must* lie along it at some point (*Fig 1*). It follows therefore that the intersection of two or more position lines obtained at the same time will mark the position of the observer's boat at the time that the bearings were taken (*Fig 2*).

It is important to recognise, however, that due to the motion of small boats, any bearing taken from them by compass is likely to be out by as much as 5° either way and so, when using this method, there is always a sector of uncertainty which must be considered when plotting a position (*Fig 3*).

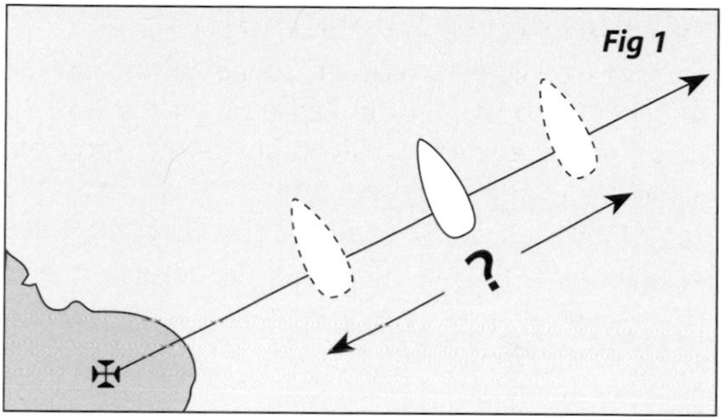
Fig 1
?

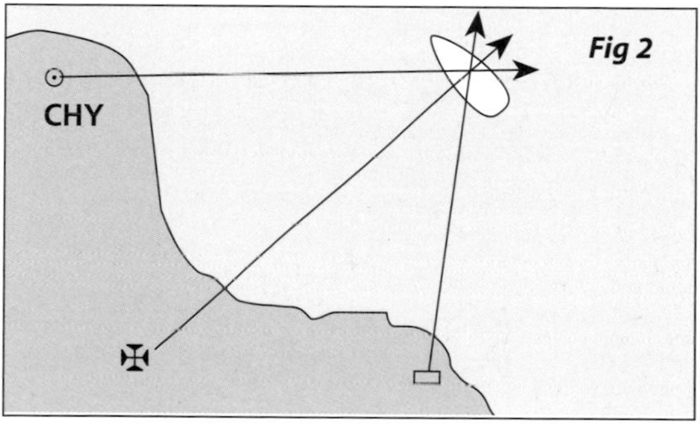
Fig 2
CHY

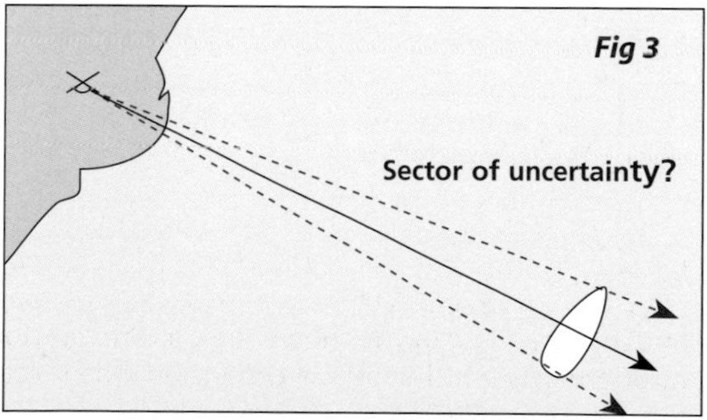
Fig 3
Sector of uncertainty?

Fixing position

Visual bearings

To fix your position by this means, identify two (preferably three) objects on the coastline that also appear on your chart (*Fig 4*).

Using a hand bearing compass

Take the bearing of each object in turn and make a note of the time and the log reading.

Convert the magnetic bearings to TRUE by applying variation as necessary and on the chart draw the appropriate bearing from each object to seaward.

Using a steering compass

Bearings can also be taken using a conveniently mounted steering compass, but bearings obtained in this manner must be corrected for both variation and deviation. Variation is taken from the chart in the usual way and deviation is read from the deviation card ***against the boat's compass heading at the time the bearing was taken***. Remember that compass deviation only changes when the boat's heading is altered (see page 15) therefore every bearing taken on that heading will have the same deviation as the steering compass.

Triangle of position or 'cocked hat'

Due to the motion of the boat, none of the bearings are likely to be completely accurate and so the intersection of three position lines will probably result in a 'cocked hat'. The size of this will give an indication of the reliability of the fix. If it is not too large, it is acceptable, but it should not be assumed that the position lies at the centre of the cocked hat, it may be close, but the wary navigator will always presume it to be situated at a point biased toward the nearest danger along the course being steered (*Fig 5*).

The three point fix

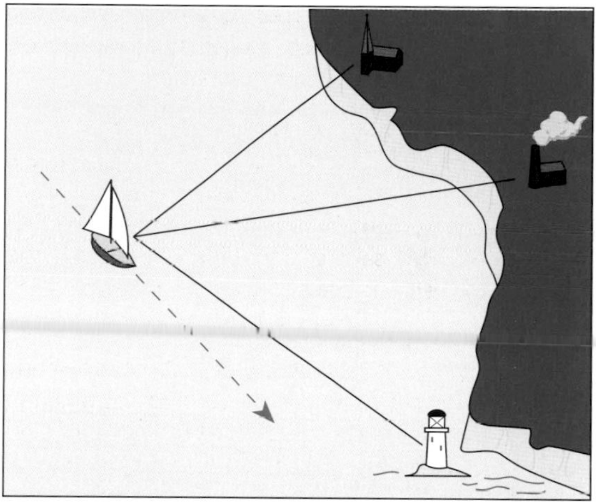

Fig 4 What you see.

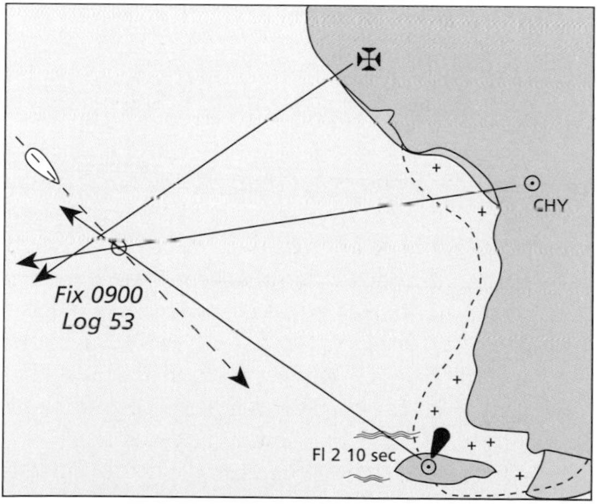

Fig 5 How it looks on the chart.

Using transits

The simplest position line is obtained when it can be seen that two *charted objects* are in transit (in line with one another). Position lines derived from transits are very accurate if they are made with two fixed and well-separated objects. Natural transits can be found by lining up towers, spires, and masts etc and can be observed without the aid of any instrument other than binoculars. All the observer needs to do is to draw a line on the chart that passes through both the objects that are seen to form a transit to be certain that his vessel lies somewhere along that line (*Fig 6*).

A reliable position fix can be obtained by combining a transit with the compass bearing of some other fixed object (*Fig 7*).

Fig 6

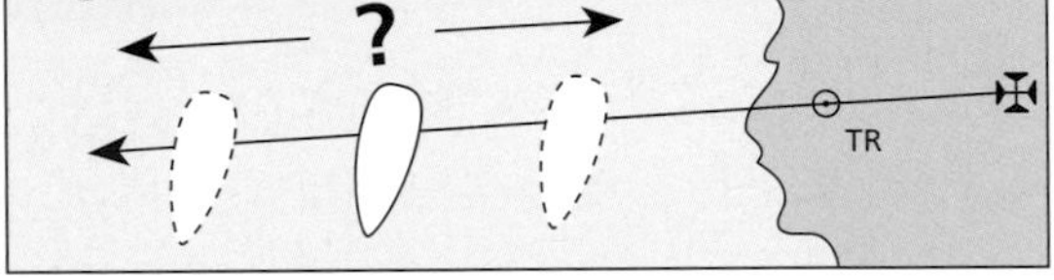

Transits are so useful to mariners that in some places, painted boards or lights have been set up in transit to provide a safe 'leading line' into harbour through narrow channels or hazardous areas (*Fig 8*). In their absence, you can sometimes create your own leading line by finding charted features that form a transit coinciding with your required course and then, by keeping them in line, make good that course. If the marks appear to drift apart when you are following a leading line, your boat has left the transit and your intended track so you must alter course to bring the objects back into line (*Fig 9*).

Note

On charts, the bearings of leading lines is always given as a 'True' bearing from seaward.

Fig 7

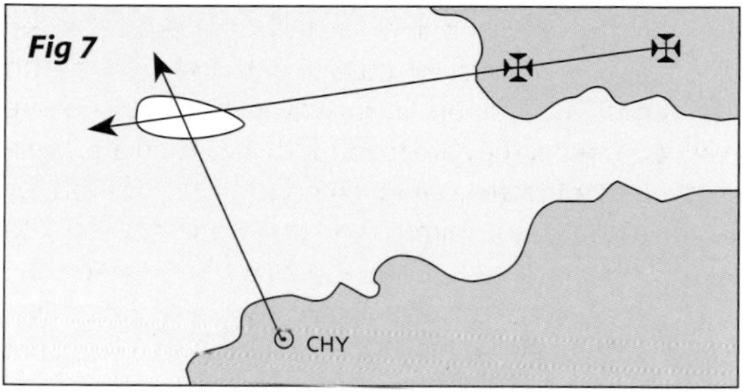

Fig 8

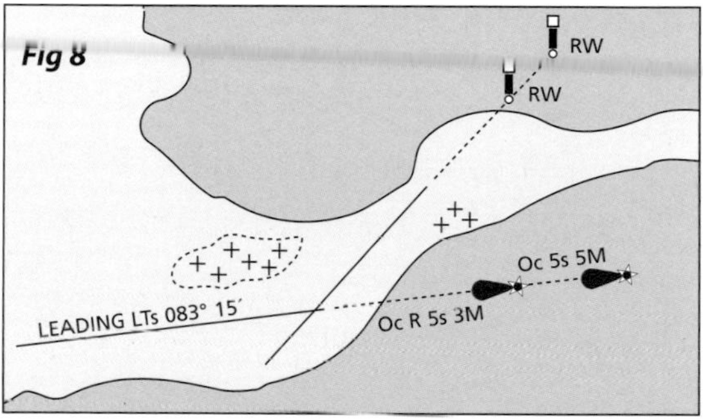

Fig 9

If the near mark appears to drift to the left of the distant mark – alter course to *port*.
If the near mark appears to drift to the right of the distant mark – alter course to *starboard*.
(If the transit is used as a 'back marker' when leaving harbour, the opposite action must be taken of course.)

Running fixes

Position lines are normally used in combination to 'fix' position and so the value of a single bearing is not always fully appreciated. When only one object is visible, however, a procedure known as the *running fix* or *transferred position line* can be used to establish your approximate position (*Fig 10*).

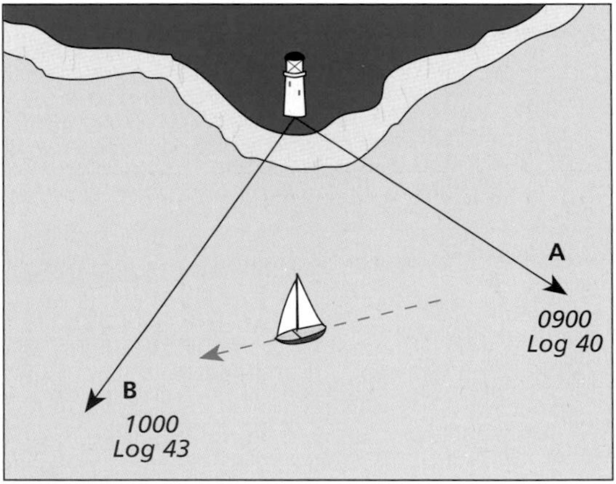

Fig 10 What you see.

Example At 0900 take the bearing of the lighthouse and read the log. One hour later, read the log again and take a second bearing on the light.

On the chart, draw both bearings **A** and **B** from the lighthouse (*Fig 11*). Then, starting from **any** point on line **A**, work out your EP by plotting your TRUE course since 0900, allowing for leeway and tidal stream. Now draw a line parallel to line **A** so that it passes through your EP and cuts line **B**. The cut on line **B** is your approximate position by running fix.

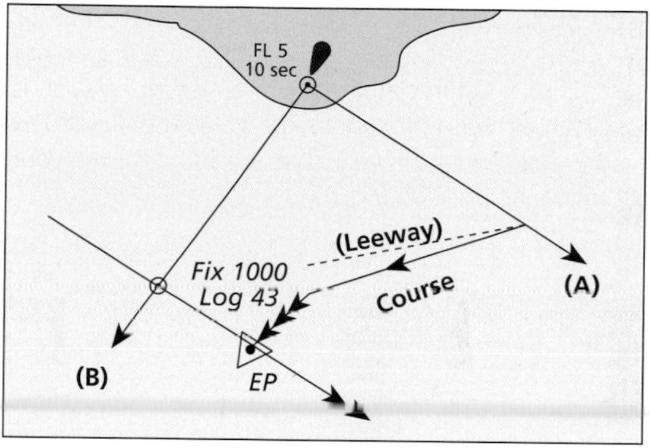

Fig 11 How it looks on the chart.

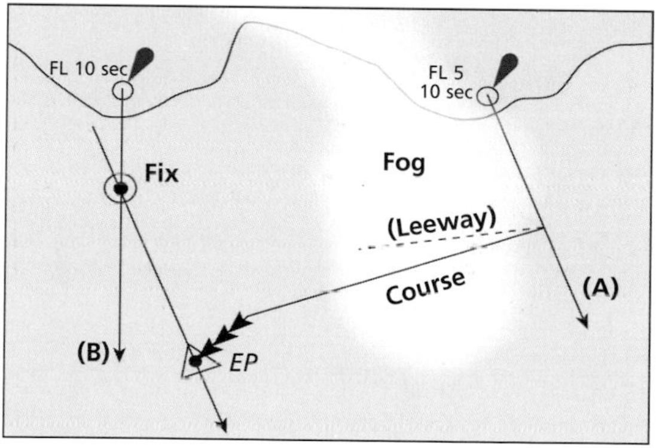

Fig 12

✷ Top tip

If for any reason (fog perhaps) the observed object (**A**) is lost to sight before a second bearing can be taken, the bearing of a different object (**B**) taken some time later can be combined with the bearing on (**A**) to provide a reasonable fix (*Fig 12*).

GPS – horizontal datums

A *horizontal datum* is a mathematical model of the Earth and the base reference for a co-ordinate system of latitude and longitude used to identify position on the Earth's surface.

All nautical charts, electronic or paper, and positions determined by GPS are based on a given horizontal datum.

A GPS receiver converts signals from orbiting satellites into a position displayed as co-ordinates of latitude and longitude, but to be of any practical value, this position needs to be related to your surroundings by plotting it on your chart. The GPS relates position to a model of a symmetrical world called WGS 84 (World Geodetic System 1984) but in reality, the Earth is not a perfect sphere and so cartographers in different parts of the world have based their charts on a variety of more suitable 'local datums' none of which quite marry up with one another, or with WGS 84, which is the default datum for most GPS receivers. It is important to understand that positions resulting from different datums can differ by several hundred metres and it is essential therefore, to ensure that your GPS and your chart are referring to the same datum.

Most GPS receivers have all the more commonly used datums built in and can be set to work on the same datum as your chart, but be careful when using a mixture of charts having different datums; it is very easy to forget to change the GPS datum when you switch to a different chart. A safer alternative might be to leave the GPS on the WGS 84 setting and carry out the necessary adjustment to position on the chart itself by following the instructions given in the note printed on the chart entitled 'Satellite derived positions'.

Waypoint navigation

Waypoints are co-ordinates taken from the chart and stored in the memory of a GPS for use as navigation reference points. A single waypoint may be used as a mark from which to plot your current position, or a series of waypoints can be positioned so as to mark successive legs of a route from one place to another.

Whenever you input a position as a waypoint, always check that the distance and bearing given by the GPS matches the distance and bearing that you measured on the chart. Any difference means that you have probably entered the latitude and longitude incorrectly?

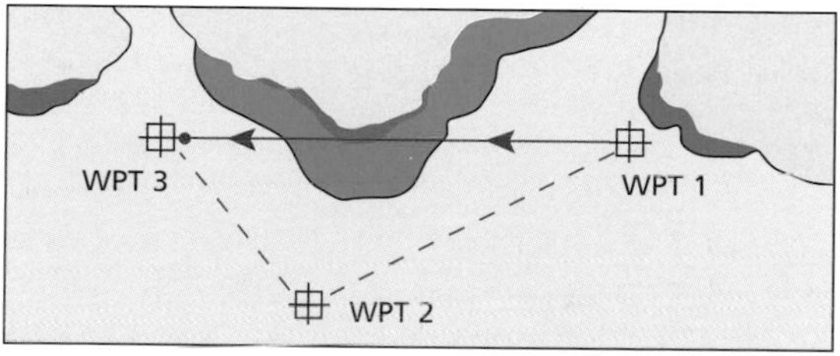

***Fig 1** Be careful when you input a waypoint into a GPS, it is easy to enter a position incorrectly, or mistakenly plan a route that takes you into danger. Here, WPT 2 has been omitted from the plan in error. The incorrect route between WPT 1 and 3 could put the boat in dangerously shallow water.*

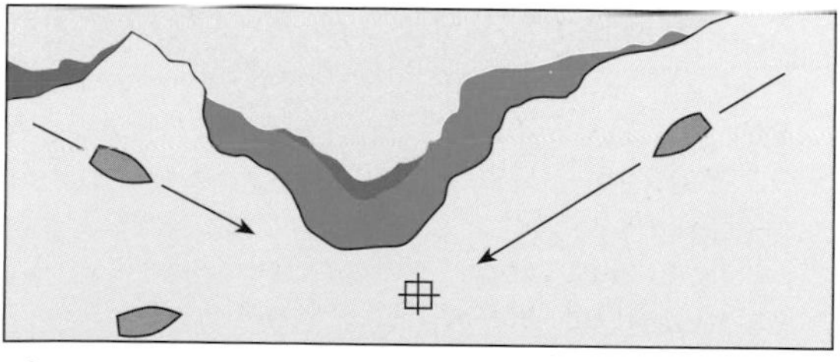

***Fig 2** It might be safer to plot a WPT near to a charted object than on it – you could hit it, and be aware that, in busy areas, other boats may be using the same WPT.*

GPS – waypoint navigation

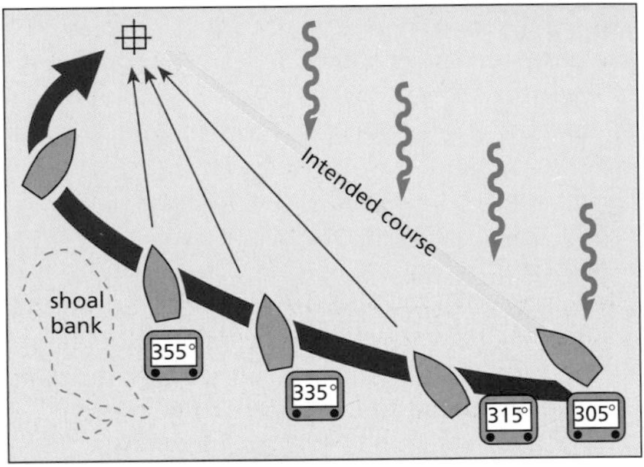

***Fig 3** A GPS does not allow for tidal streams so always pre-plan the course to steer. If you repeatedly alter course to steer to a mark using bearings given by your GPS you will sail further and might put your boat in danger.*

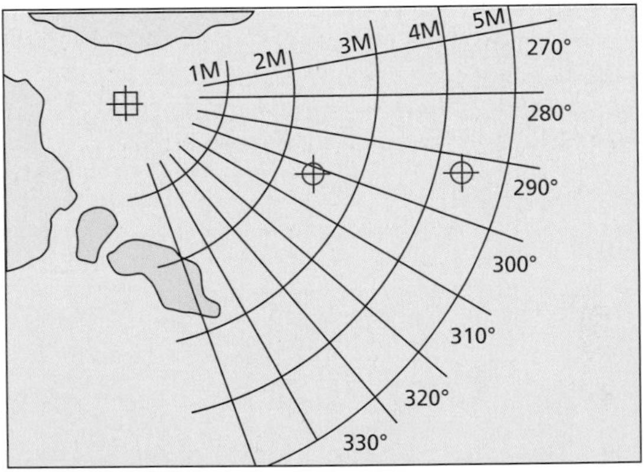

***Fig 4** Traditional plotting methods can be difficult on fast-moving boats. Pre-plan your navigation by drawing a web of ranges and bearings from your key waypoint, then periodically check its range and bearing by GPS to see your changing position within the web as you approach.*

GPS – position by range and bearing

It is often easier to plot your position more accurately using the GPS bearing and distance display than by taking co-ordinates from the latitude and longitude readout and transferring them onto the chart.

You needn't use just the waypoint you are aiming for to get a range and bearing. An alternative is to store the position at the centre of one of the chart's compass roses as a random waypoint in the GPS. You can then plot its bearing quickly and accurately, whenever you want to, and you don't even need a plotter to do this. Any straight edge will do because it can be lined up directly on the compass rose itself, but do remember to read the bearing from the *opposite* side of the rose as the bearing is *to* the waypoint and then step off the distance from the *centre* of the rose – *not* the edge.

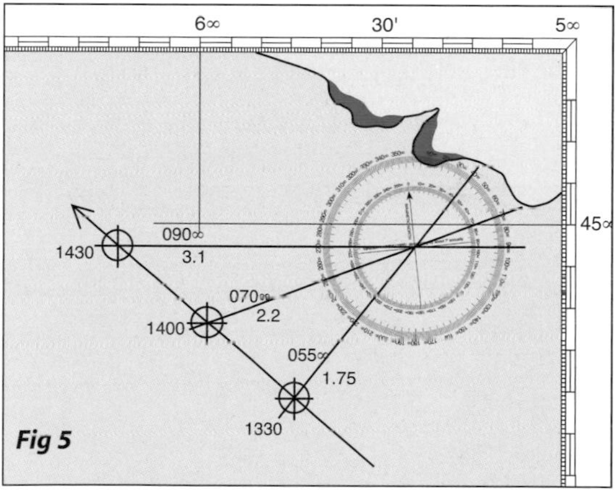

Fig 5

A second GPS bearing on a similarly chosen arbitrary position will help to confirm the fix, or better still, try to obtain a non-GPS cross check such as a depth sounding or visual bearing to confirm the position.

GPS – position by Lat and Long

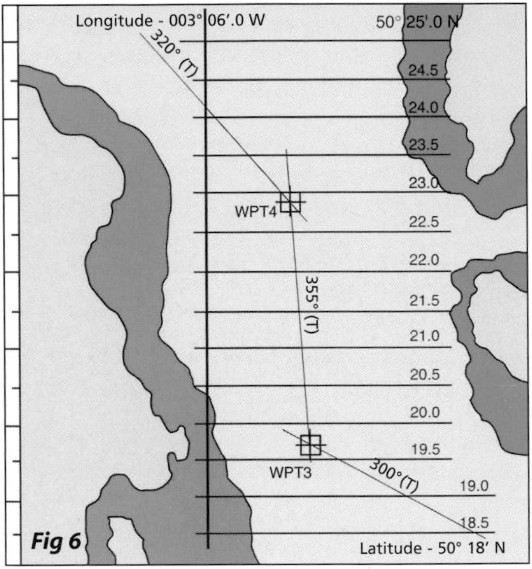

Fig 6

Pre-planning for rapid plotting of position when 'sea room' or visibility is limited can be especially useful on fast boats where traditional chartwork is difficult.

Using this method, you have only one co-ordinate to plot and accuracy is good since you will be using only the basic GPS latitude and longitude readout.

First, draw a meridian on the chart near to your intended ground track, and *clear of all dangers*. From that meridian mark off the appropriate part of the latitude scale so that it crosses your ground track; then en-route every time the GPS shows that you are crossing one of the marked latitudes, make a note of the corresponding longitude and the time, and you will be able to plot your position as often as you wish.

If your intended track is more east to west, draw in a parallel of latitude and mark it up with the lines of longitude that you expect to cross.

GPS – crosstrack and range to waypoint

A pre-prepared range and XTE (cross track error) 'ladder' is an ideal quick plotting method for fast boats when making longer coastal passages.

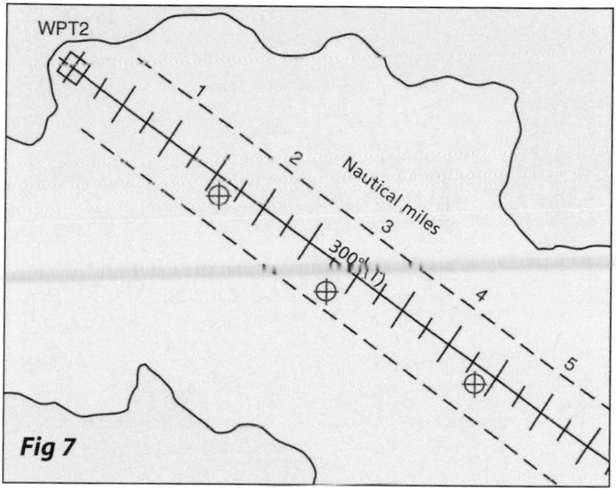

Fig 7

Draw your intended track on the chart in the usual way but with a scale of distance to the waypoint marked along it. Next draw lines parallel to the track, *well clear of any hazard*, to mark the limits of acceptable cross track error on either side.

A series of range and XTE readings taken from the GPS display at regular intervals will then help you to stay within your self-imposed limits, and maintain a record on the chart of your vessel's progress along the desired track. **Note**: You cannot get a XTE reading unless your course lies between two waypoints.

✱ **Top tip** Find the correct course to steer before you set off (see page 38) especially if tidal streams are strong. This will ensure that you will be counter-acting the tide from the outset rather than waiting until your boat has been pushed off course before you can begin to work out the offset to apply.

GPS – sailing to windward

Destination to windward

When your destination lies directly upwind of the boat it becomes necessary to beat towards it by sailing close hauled on alternate tacks, preferably keeping within 10° to 15° of the downwind line so as to be well placed to take advantage of any favourable windshifts.

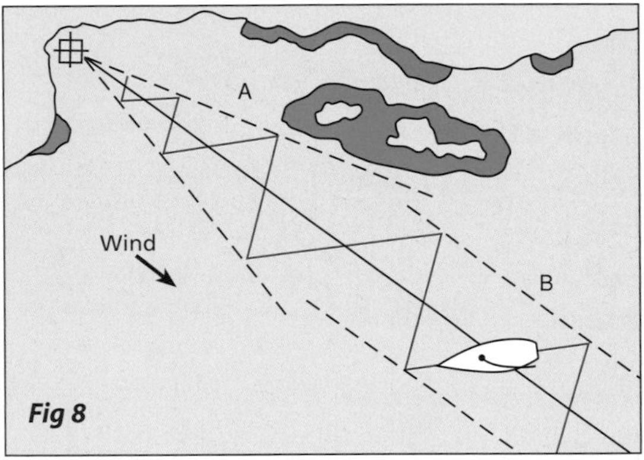

Fig 8

To do this, draw the downwind line on the chart then construct a 'cone' by drawing lines to either side of it, radiating about 10° from the destination but clear of all off-lying dangers (**A**). Set off on the tack that points more directly towards your destination and using GPS, tack whenever the bearing to the mark is 10° to either side of the direct track.

If you are facing a very long beat to windward, start by sailing along a corridor formed by 'tack limiting lines' set at a convenient distance to each side of the downwind line (**B**). Using the XTE function, your boat's position will be shown at right angles to the downwind line enabling you to tack when either of the limit lines is reached, until you are closer to your destination and can use GPS bearings on the mark to tack within the limits of the cone.

GPS – laying the windward mark

When you are nearing your destination and the wind and tide are unlikely to change appreciably, you can use your GPS to tell you when to make the final tack to 'lay the mark' (*Fig 9*).

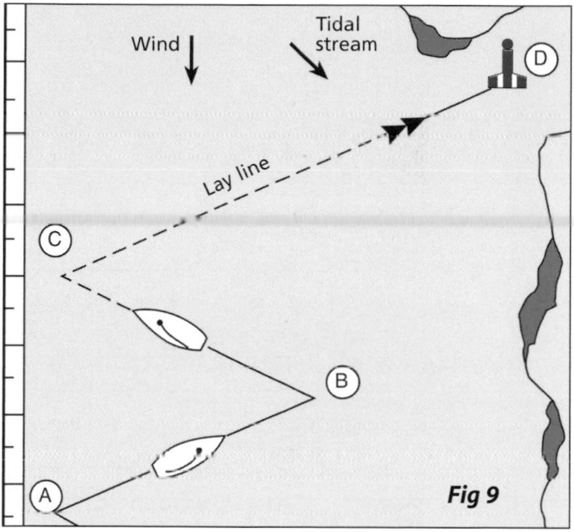

Fig 9

You expect to head for the fairway buoy on port tack, so make a note of the COG (ground track) shown by the GPS as you head for point B on the previous port tack. Enter the position of the buoy into the GPS as a waypoint and select it with the GO-TO function. The GPS will then show a continuously changing bearing to the waypoint as you sail on starboard tack from B towards C. When the bearing of the waypoint matches that of the ground track between A and B, you will have reached the theoretical point at which you should tack onto port and head for the buoy although to be sure, it might pay to hold your starboard tack for just a while longer. (See page 46 for the 'traditional' method.)

GPS – clearing bearings

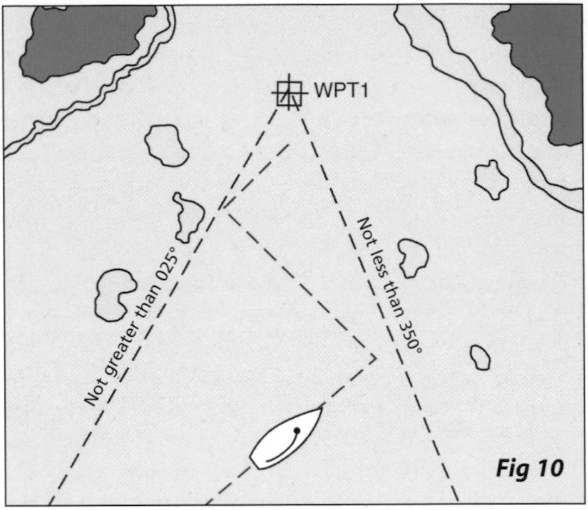

Fig 10

If you need to tack into a harbour or an anchorage that has dangers to either side of the entrance, look at the chart and find a suitable position within the harbour and enter it into the GPS as a waypoint. Draw lines radiating from the waypoint that will keep you well clear of any dangers, then when sailing in, you can tack whenever the GPS bearing to the waypoint matches either of the clearing bearings plotted on the chart.

A power-driven vessel doesn't usually need to tack of course unless perhaps, for reasons of comfort or safety, its skipper decides to adopt a tacking procedure in order to take oncoming waves at an angle rather than head on, otherwise he can adopt a similar strategy to the sailboat skipper and avoid lateral dangers by following a direct bearing to the waypoint whilst taking care not to stray beyond clearing bearings set to either side.

Chart plotters

Unlike GPS receivers that must be used in conjunction with a paper chart, an electronic chart plotter, when interfaced with GPS, will display your boat's continuously updated position on an electronic representation of a nautical chart and enable you to see at a glance where you are in relation to your surroundings. With most plotters, you can also enter waypoints, measure direction and distance, and plan a course or route 'on screen'.

Chart plotters are generally either PC driven software systems, whose main benefit is a potentially large display, or a unit specifically designed for the marine environment, and having a customised control panel and integral software, but with a comparatively small screen.

Electronic charts are available in either *raster* or *vector* formats. Basically, vector charts are layered graphic representations of the data shown on a paper chart and each layer can be selected and viewed separately allowing you to change the level of information you want, whereas raster charts are exact photographic images of paper charts and as such, the information on them cannot be changed or manipulated.

There is a general misconception that electronic charts are more accurate than paper charts but in fact, since all electronic charts are digitised from conventional paper charts, whichever system you use – raster or vector, the electronic data is no better than that of the paper chart source.

✱ Top tip

If your primary navigation is by GPS, bear in mind that it could be knocked out by power, aerial, or satellite failure. Always maintain a record of your GPS position in the log and have the appropriate paper charts available too.

The Automatic Identification System

Collision avoidance

Radar has long been a valuable aid to pilotage in fog and darkness and the only electronic navigation aid that could be used for collision avoidance. One negative aspect of radar though, is the inability to positively identify a specific radar target when multiple contacts are being tracked, especially at night when it is impossible to verify a vessel's identity visually.

This difficulty has now been largely overcome with the advent of the Automatic Identification System (AIS) – a shipboard VHF transponder system which enables ships to exchange ID, position, course, speed and other essential data with other nearby AIS equipped ships and shore stations via a common VHF radio channel.

AIS works autonomously, continuously transmitting data to all other AIS equipped vessels within VHF range. The ship's position, course, speed and other navigational data is fed into the AIS by the ship's interfaced sensors where it is formatted and transmitted as a short 'data burst' on a dedicated VHF radio channel. When this data is received by other AIS equipped ships, it is automatically decoded and can be displayed in graphic and text format. Optionally, the data may also be fed to the ship's radar plotting system to provide AIS tags for radar targets. The usefulness of this data decays rapidly with time of course, so it is continually updated by the AIS and retransmitted every few seconds.

At present, AIS is only mandatory for large commercial vessels subject to the SOLAS convention and small vessels such as workboats, fishing vessels and pleasure craft are not required to have the system, but its potential to make a significant contribution to safety and collision avoidance makes it a highly desirable proposition for any small craft.

It is not practical to install full commercial Class A AIS sets in small craft, however, as they are unlikely to be equipped with type approved gyro-compasses or GPS sets so, for the small boat owner, the choice is between either a Class B AIS set or a 'receive only' unit such as NASA Marine Instruments' relatively inexpensive 'AIS Radar' (*Fig 1*). This is a stand alone unit which will plot the position and track of all AIS carrying vessels within normal VHF range and display them relative to the user's position. The user can then select any vessel on the screen and its AIS data will be displayed alongside.

Naval vessels are not obliged to transmit on AIS.

Fig 1 AIS radar set made by NASA Marine Instruments.

Standard ports

In the almanac, each standard port is given its own tide table and tidal curves. The time and height of high and low water is read directly from the table and the curves are used to find the height of tide at any other time between high and low water, for example:

On 1 May at Walton-on-the-Naze

a) What will the height of tide be at 1100 GMT?
and

b) At what time will the tide reach a height of 1·75m?

- First, mark up the graph with the Walton high and low water times and heights and join the heights with a line as shown.
- Now compare the predicted range of tide with the mean ranges at springs and neaps and decide which curve to use or whether to interpolate between them (see page 74).

To answer (a) Enter the graph at the required time – 1100 and proceed as shown by the **red** line to find the height of tide at this time: **2·9m approx**.

To answer (b) Enter the graph at the required height of 1·75m and proceed as shown by the **blue** line to find the time at which this height will occur: **0926 GMT approx**.

- The height found by graph when added to the depth shown on the chart is the actual depth at that place.
- A drying height shown on the chart when subtracted from the height found by graph will be the depth (if any) at that place.

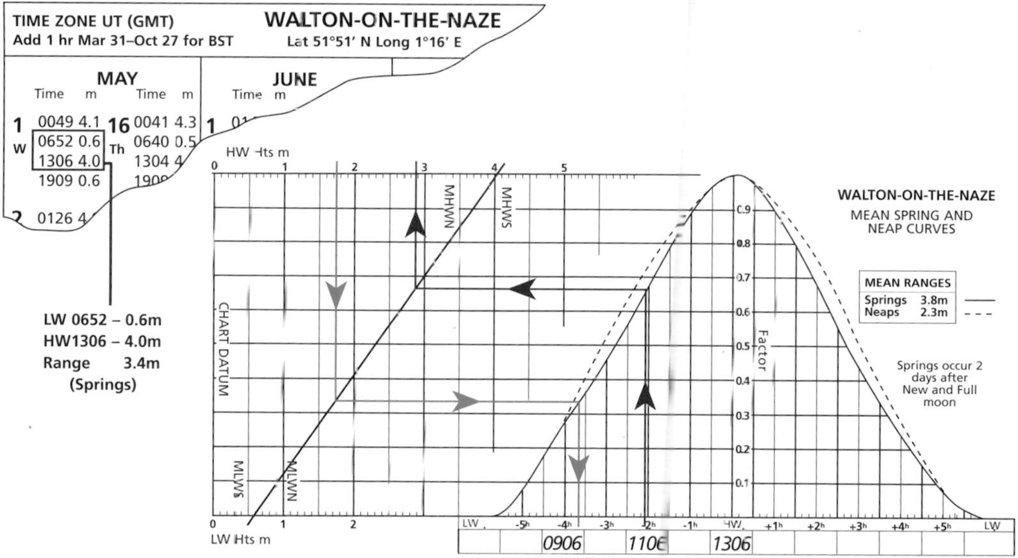
TIME ZONE UT (GMT)
Add 1 hr Mar 31–Oct 27 for BST
WALTON-ON-THE-NAZE
Lat 51°51′ N Long 1°16′ E
MAY
JUNE
Time m
1 W 0049 4.1 0652 0.6 1306 4.0 1909 0.6
16 Th 0041 4.3 0640 0.5
2 0126
LW 0652 – 0.6m
HW1306 – 4.0m
Range 3.4m
(Springs)
HW Hts m
LW Hts m
CHART DATUM
MHWS
MHWN
MLWN
MLWS
Factor
WALTON-ON-THE-NAZE
MEAN SPRING AND
NEAP CURVES
MEAN RANGES
Springs 3.8m
Neaps 2.3m
Springs occur 2 days after New and Full moon
LW -5h -4h -3h -2h -1h HW +1h +2h +3h +4h +5h LW
0906
1106
1306

Secondary ports

Tidal differences

Tidal predictions are published in full for selected places called standard ports, but tidal data for smaller secondary ports must be found by applying local corrections – tabulated in the almanac as 'differences' – to the standard port times and heights, for example:

STANDARD PORT: WALTON-ON-THE NAZE

TIMES				HEIGHTS (Metres)			
HW		LW		MHWS	MHWN	MLWN	MLWS
0000 AND 1200	0600 AND 1800	0500 AND 1700	1100 AND 2300	4.2	3.4	1.1	0.4
DIFFERENCES – BRADWELL							
+0035	+0023	+0047	+0004	+1.1	+0.8	+0.2	+0.1

Time differences

The table is saying that if HW at Walton occurs at either 0000 or 1200 then HW at Bradwell will be 35 minutes later. Alternatively if HW Walton is either 0600 or 1800 then it will occur 23 minutes later at Bradwell.

Similarly if LW occurs at Walton at either 0500 or 1700, LW at Bradwell will be 47 minutes later, but only 4 minutes later if LW Walton is either 1100 or 2300.

▸▸ Important Note

Tide tables give times of high and low water in the standard – or *zone time* of the port. For all UK ports this is:

Time zone zero. Greenwich Mean Time (GMT/UT).

Time zones

The relevant time zone is shown at the top of each tide table (see page 71) and the sign +/– shows how the time zone correction should be applied to convert local time to GMT, ie:

Calais time zone – 0100 (Fr standard time).
Subtract one hour for GMT

Many countries operate 'Summer Time' and during British Summer Time (BST) one hour should be added to tabulated GMT times. When working out times for secondary ports, however, this correction should ***not*** be made until all other calculations are complete; otherwise serious inaccuracy will result because the time differences for the secondary port are related to the times of high and low water at the standard port which are given in GMT.

Height differences

These are applied in much the same way as time differences, and in this instance the table says that when the height of HW at Walton is either 4·2 or 3·4m it will be 1·1 or 0·8m higher respectively at Bradwell and when LW at Walton is either 1.1 or 0.4m, then, at Bradwell, it will be 0.2 or 0.1m higher respectively.

When the tidal predictions for the day do not coincide exactly with the times and heights specified in the table of differences, interpolation is necessary between the differences to be applied for that port. This can usually be carried out quite satisfactorily 'by eye' but a simple free hand graph is more accurate if the magnitude of the differences varies greatly. See page 75.

Secondary ports

Interpolation - tidal differences

Example On a chosen day, HW Walton is 1405 3·8m. It can be seen that 1405 falls between the reference times of 1200 and 1800 on the table of differences (see page 72), therefore the exact difference which has to be applied lies proportionally between +35 to +23min (about +30min by eye).

To be more accurate

- Draw a graph as shown with the Walton reference times 1200 to 1800 along one side and their corresponding differences for Bradwell +35 to +23min along the opposite side (see note on page 75).
- Close the triangle by drawing a line A–B between the last units on upper and lower lines.
- Enter the graph with HW Walton 1405 and draw a line ***parallel to line A–B*** to cut the lower line where the difference to be applied can now be read off (+31min).

The height of HW at Walton, 3·8, falls between 4·2 and 3·4m on the table of differences which means that the difference to apply lies between 1·1 and 0·8m.

The precise difference could be found by constructing another graph with reference heights along one side and the corresponding differences along the other but in this instance as the range of difference is so small (0.3m) interpolation by eye should be quite adequate.

Interpolation of differences

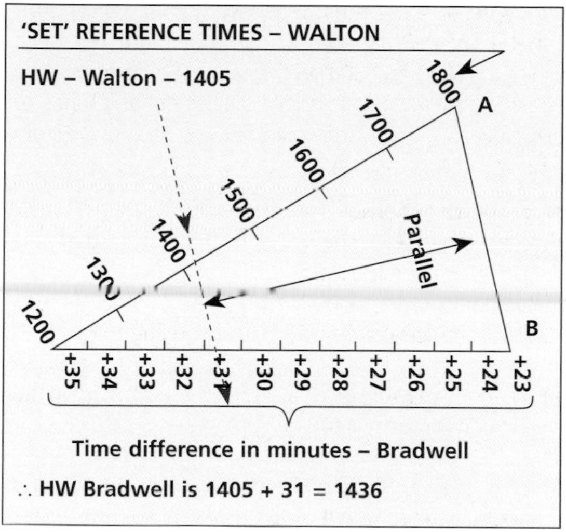

The triangle may be drawn to *any* appropriate size and *any* suitable scale may be used, but it is ***essential*** to keep the reference times and their corresponding differences in the correct relationship as shown.

✷ Top tip

Tidal height predictions for any given place are based upon the average height of tide recorded at that place over a long period of time. Usually these predictions are very good but it is always best to allow a generous margin for error whenever you are calculating clearance over an obstruction.

Secondary ports

Secondary ports – intermediate heights

The time and height of high and low water at a secondary port is obtained by applying the differences tabulated in the almanac to the standard port's tidal predictions.

Secondary ports do not usually have their own tidal curves, so when the height of tide at any time between that of high and low water at a secondary port is required, the curve belonging to the standard port is used after first marking it up with the corrected tidal information (both times and height) for the secondary port as shown below.

	(Time) HW	LW	(Height) HW	LW
Walton =	**1200**	**1700**	**4.2m**	**0.4m**
Differences =	**+35**	**+47**	**+1.1**	**+0.1**
Bradwell =	**1235**	**1747**	**5.3**	**0.5**

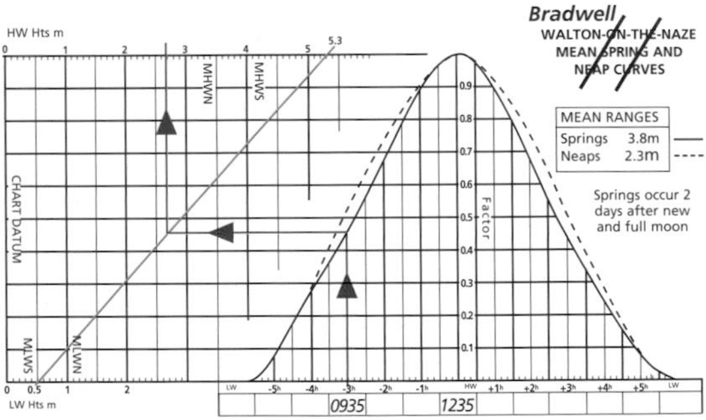

When the secondary port tidal data has been entered onto the standard port graph, heights of tide at intermediate time eg 0935 at the secondary port can quickly be found by following the procedure detailed on page 70.

Rule of Twelfths

This rule gives a rough guide to the height* of a *semi-diurnal tide* at times between high and low water by assuming that the tidal cycle is symmetrical and that the duration of rise or fall is approximately six hours. Unfortunately the tide does not rise or fall evenly for each hour between high and low water and it also varies from place to place. For this reason, heights found by this rule are *very approximate* and should be used with great caution and with a generous margin for error.

The rule states that the rate of rise or fall is:
During the first hour 1⁄12 of the range
During the second hour 2⁄12 of the range
During the third hour 3⁄12 of the range
During the fourth hour 3⁄12 of the range
During the fifth hour 2⁄12 of the range
During the sixth hour 1⁄12 of the range

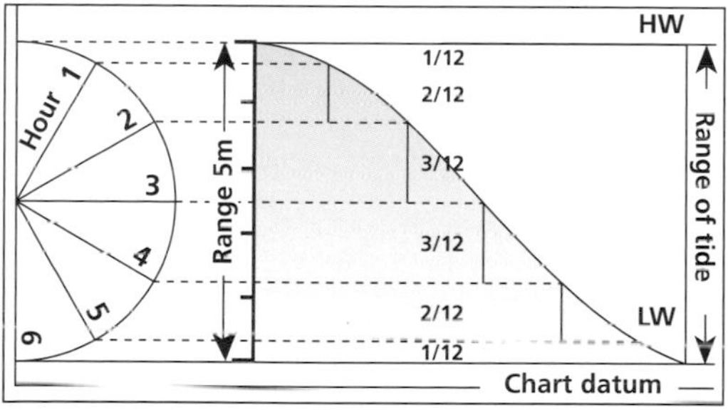

*The rise or fall of tide found by this rule must then be applied to the predicted height of high or low water as appropriate, to obtain the height of tide above chart datum.

✷ Top tip

The range of the tide is the vertical difference in height between successive high and low waters. If you draw the range of tide to scale across the clock face as shown, the 'state of the tide' at any given time can be seen at a glance.

Anomalies – South coast

Many factors, such as the depth of water or size and configuration of the coast, can affect the tide and no two places have exactly the same tidal pattern. Some places have exceptionally high or low tides and others like the Baltic or Mediterranean seas have little or no tide at all. In the British Isles, unusual double high waters occur in the region between Swanage and Selsey where times of LW are more easily defined than HW times; so special tidal curves with times relative to *low water* are used for this area. In all other respects, the method of finding heights of tide at intermediate times with these curves is identical to that used for normal secondary ports except that, as the tides at some of these places cannot be defined properly by two curves, a third 'critical' curve has been introduced for the range of tide at the standard port – Portsmouth. Any necessary interpolation should take place between this third curve and either the spring or neap curve as appropriate , for example:

Find height of tide at Lymington at 2130 BST when at the standard port tidal predictions are:

LW 1905 BST – 1·1m
HW 0204 BST – 4·5m

1 Find the tidal data for Lymington by applying the differences to Portsmouth in the usual way.

2 Mark the corrected time and heights found onto the Lymington graph and join the heights with a line in the normal way.

3 Enter the graph at the time required (2130 BST), and proceed as shown by the red line to obtain the height of tide at this time.

Anomalies – South coast

South Coast – Lymington and Yarmouth

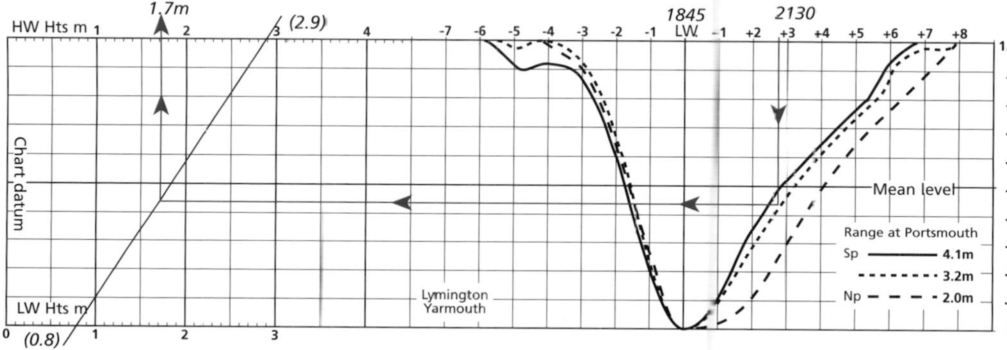

	LW		HW		
Portsmouth predictions	1905 BST	1.1m	——	4.5m	(Range 3.4m)
Diffs (interpolated)	– 20 min	–0.3m		–1.6m	
Tides at Lymington	1845 BST	0.8m		2.9m	

(Height of tide at 2130 = 1.7m approx)

Note In this example, the range of tide at Portsmouth is very close to that of the critical curve so interpolation is between the critical curve and the spring curve.

Reduction to soundings

Height of tide and depth of water

When a sounding is taken in tidal waters, it cannot be related to the depths which are shown on the chart until the prevailing height of tide at that place has been established and subtracted from the sounding.

This procedure is called *reduction to soundings* and forms an important part of several tidal calculations including the confirmation of an estimated position or to assist in pilotage when 'running a line of soundings'.

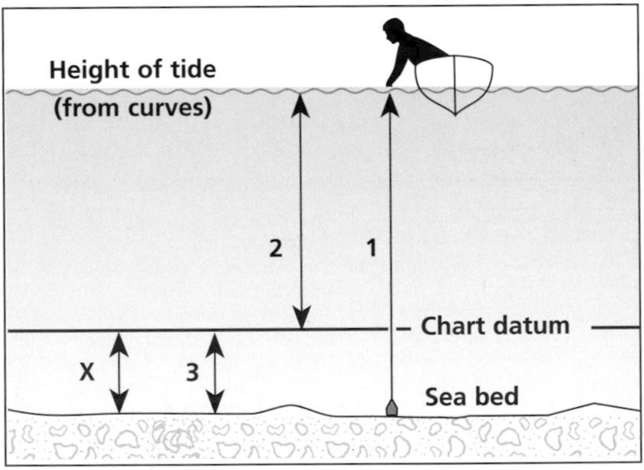

Key

1 Sounding taken
2 Minus height of tide
3 Gives the reduced sounding
X Charted sounding

NB 3 and X should more or less agree if your EP is correct.

Reduction to soundings

Height of tide reduced to soundings using uncalibrated echo sounder

Many echo sounders can be adjusted to measure depth either from the waterline or from below the keel. If yours is one of the simpler sounders that only measures depth below the transducer, you will need to allow for this in your calculations.

1 Echo sounder reading	
2 Plus distance transducer to waterline	
3 Gives the actual depth	
4 Minus height of tide	
5 Gives the reduced sounding	

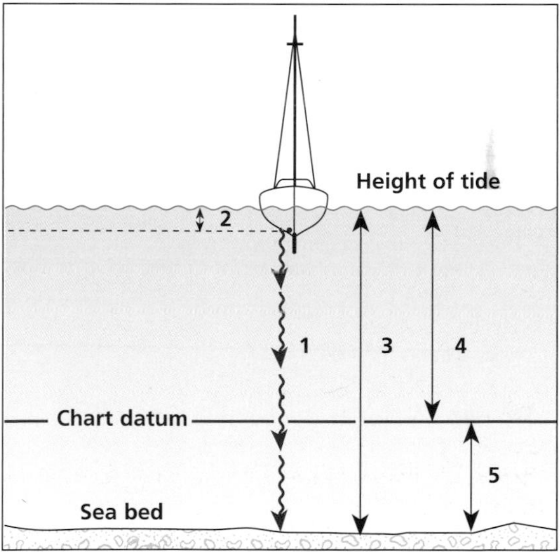

Compare the reduced sounding obtained to the charted sounding at your EP to confirm the position.

Finding depth to anchor

Will there be enough water at low tide?

This is a quick and easy way of finding the depth in which to anchor without calculation.

Preparation

1 Find the times and heights of high and low water for the area you are in and plot the heights on your nearest standard port tidal curve as line **A**.

2 Mark on the LW line the minimum depth at which you want to be afloat (draught plus safety margin) and from this point draw a line **B** ***parallel*** to line **A**.

From now on line **A** is disregarded and anytime you want to anchor, the required depth can be read off quickly by reference to line **B**.

Example If HW at Walton is 3·5m at 1200 and LW is 0·8m at 1800, plot this on the curve as line **A**.

Now mark your minimum anchoring depth (say 2m) on the LW line and from it draw line **B** ***parallel*** to line **A**.

When you want to anchor, just check the time and draw a line up to the appropriate curve, across to line **B** then up or down to find the safest minimum depth to drop anchor. In this instance – at 0920 – just circle round until your echo sounder reads 3·6m or more.

▶▶ Note

If your anchor cable is all chain you should veer 4 x max depth of water expected but if using rope with a chain leader, you should veer at least 6 x max depth of water expected.

Finding depth to anchor

Predictions:	HW 1200	3.5	Range 2.7
	LW 1800	0.8	
Time required:	0920		Min depth required: 2m

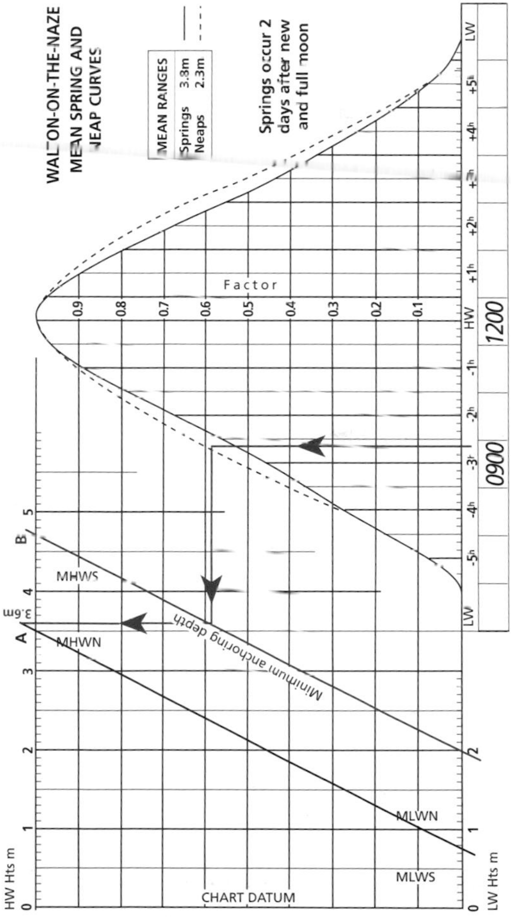

Anchoring – depth by echo sounder

Finding depth by echo sounder to avoid going aground at LW

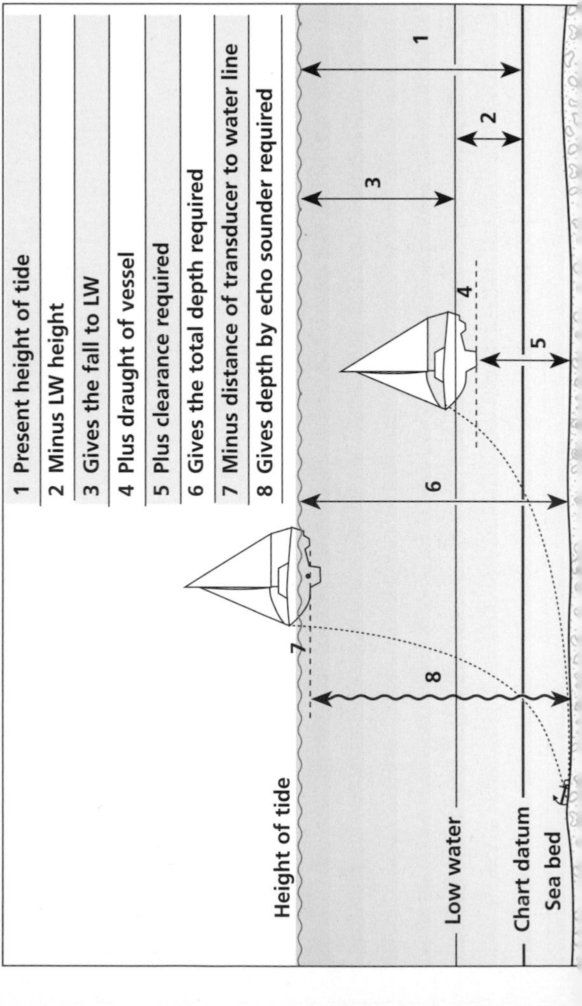

Depth and clearance below the keel

To find clearance at LW using handline and lead

1	Depth by handline	
2	Minus present height of tide	
3	Gives depth below chart datum	
4	Plus height of next LW	
5	Gives depth at LW	
6	Minus draught of vessel	
7	Gives clearance at LW	

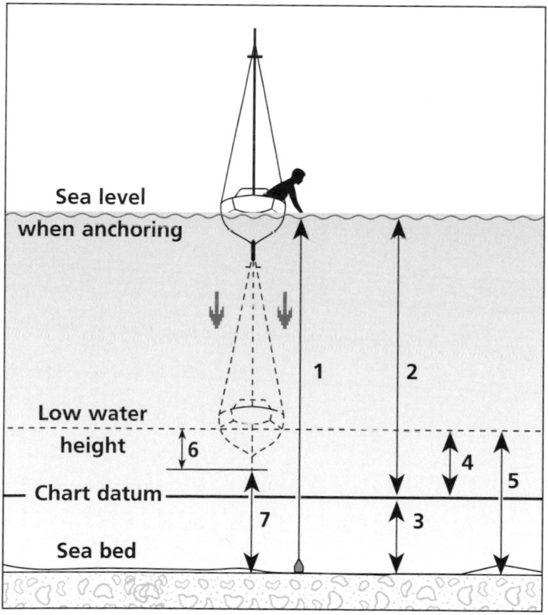

Depth and clearance below the keel

To find clearance at low water using echo sounder

1 Echo sounder reading	
2 Plus distance – transducer to waterline	
3 Gives true depth of water	
4 Minus present height of tide	
5 Gives depth below chart datum	
6 Plus height of next LW	
7 Gives depth at LW	
8 Minus draught of vessel	
9 Gives clearance at LW	

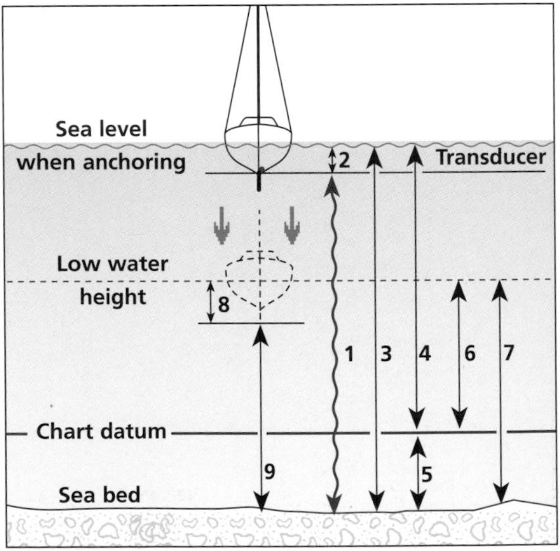

Depth and clearance below the keel

What is the depth beneath my keel?

1 Present height of tide	
2 Plus charted sounding	
3 Gives total depth of water	
4 Minus draught of vessel	
5 Gives depth below the keel	

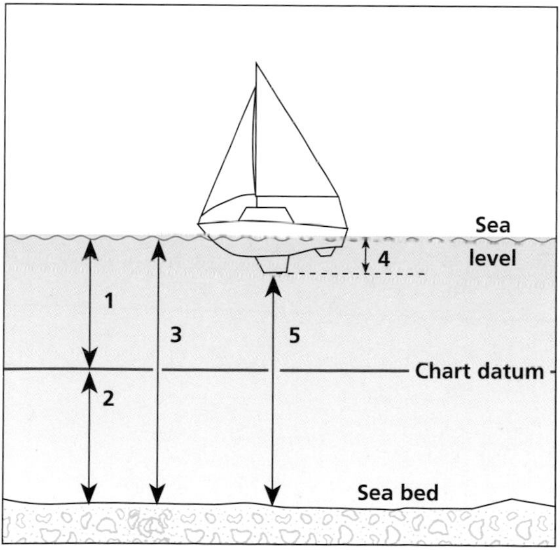

Use tidal curve to calculate the present height of the tide

Depth and clearance below the keel

Height of tide required to clear a bank or bar

1 Draught of the vessel	
2 Plus clearance required	
3 Gives total depth required	
4 Minus charted sounding	
5 Gives height of tide required	

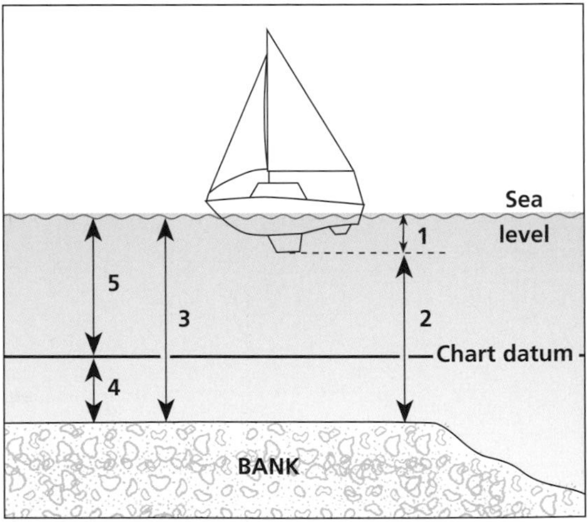

Use tidal curve to find the time at which height required will occur.

Depth and clearance below the keel

Height of tide required to clear a charted drying height

1 Draught of the vessel	
2 Plus clearance required	
3 Plus charted drying height	
4 Gives height of tide required	

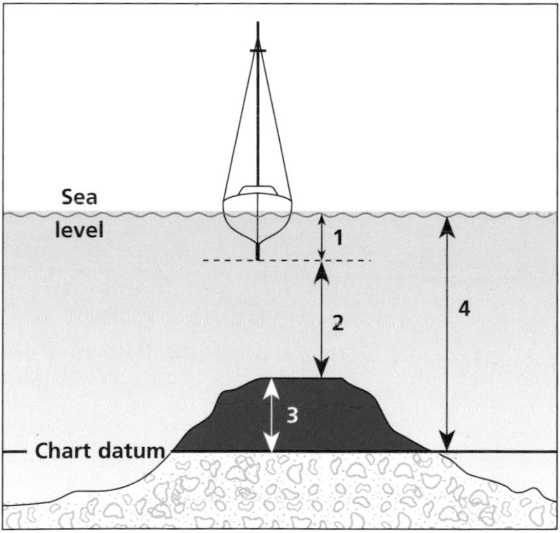

Use tidal curve to find the time at which the required height will occur.

Depth and clearance below the keel

Will my vessel clear a charted drying height?

1 Present height of tide	
2 Minus drying height	
3 Gives actual depth of water	
4 Minus draught of vessel	
5 Gives clearance beneath the keel	

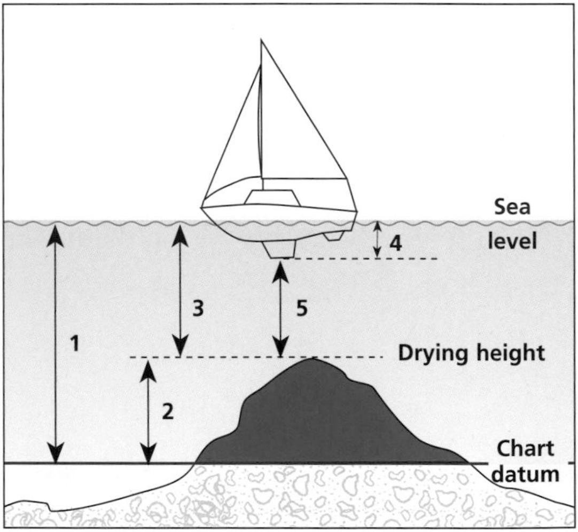

On a falling tide: ***use tidal curve to find the latest time to cross in safety.***

On a rising tide: ***use tidal curve to find the time at which the required height will occur.***

The height of all charted terrestrial features other than drying heights are measured from the level of MHWS tides.

If the height of MHWS above chart datum is known it is possible to find the actual height of the feature above sea level by adding its charted height to the level of MHWS at that place and then subtracting the height of tide at the time from the total (*Fig 1*).

When the height of the feature has been established a *distance off* can be calculated in daytime by vertical sextant angle (see page 96) or at night by 'rising or dipping' of the light (see page 92).

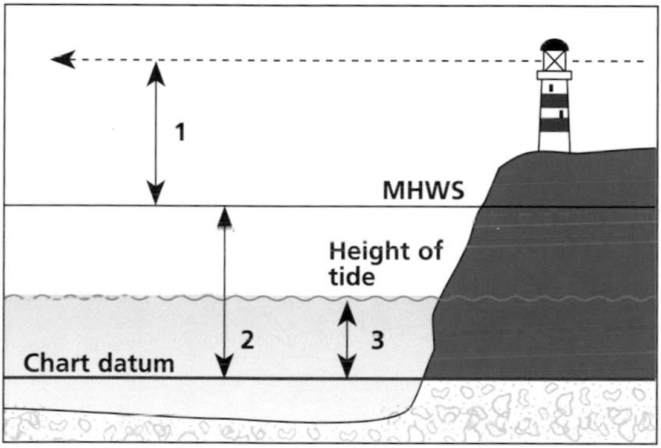

Fig 1

1	Charted height of light	20m
2	Plus height of MHWS	6m
3	Gives the height above chart datum	26m
4	Minus the height of tide	2m
5	Gives the height above sea level	24m

Rising or dipping lights

An approximate distance off may be obtained at night when approaching land by observing the point at which a light first appears above the horizon or, conversely, when leaving the coast by noting the point at which it is on the verge of disappearing below the horizon.

This distance, which is dependant upon the 'height of eye' of the observer and the elevation of the light is called the *geographical range of the light* and is the maximum distance at which a light with sufficient intensity can be seen when limited only by the curvature of the Earth (*Fig 2*).

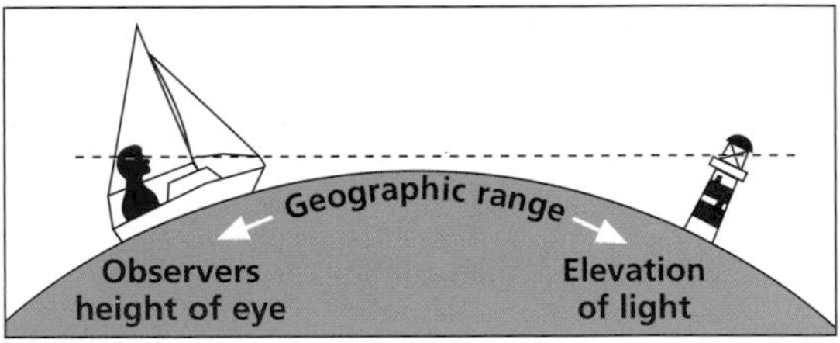

Fig 2

The observed height of the light above sea level together with the height of eye of the observer above sea level, is referred to the appropriate table in a nautical almanac to obtain a distance off.

If tables are unavailable, a reliable distance off can be obtained with the formula:

$$\sqrt{\text{Ht of eye (m)}} \text{ plus } \sqrt{\text{Ht of light (m)}} \times 2.075$$

$$\sqrt{\text{Ht of eye (ft)}} \text{ plus } \sqrt{\text{Ht of light (ft)}} \times 1.15$$

$$= \text{Distance off in nautical miles}$$

1 Charted height of light	
2 Plus level of MHWS	
3 Gives height of light above chart datum	
4 Minus height of tide prevailing	
5 Gives height of light above sea level	

Now refer the height of the light found, together with the observer's height of eye, to the Range of Lights table on page 201 to obtain the 'distance off' (*Fig 3*).

The bearing of the light, if taken at the same time will provide the remaining information needed to acquire a reasonable 'fix'.

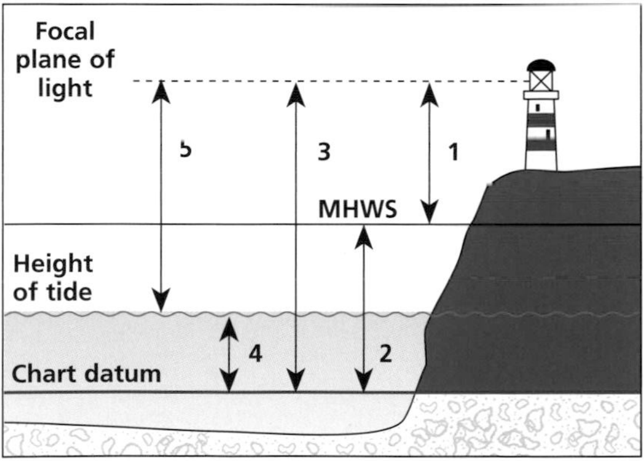

Fig 3

Index error

When coastal sailing, the sextant can be used to fix the boat's position by means of either vertical or horizontal angles of charted objects such as lighthouses etc. Before using it for this purpose, the sextant should be adjusted according to the maker's instructions. Any residual error in the instrument after this is known as *index error* and its value must be applied as a correction to all future sextant readings.

To find the index error

1. Clamp index bar and micrometer drum at zero.
2. Hold the sextant vertically and sight a clear, distant horizon turning the drum until the true and reflected horizons form a single unbroken line.
3. The sextant reading indicates the index error.
4. If the reading is on the 'plus' side of zero it must be subtracted as a correction.
5. If the reading is on the negative side of zero it must be added.

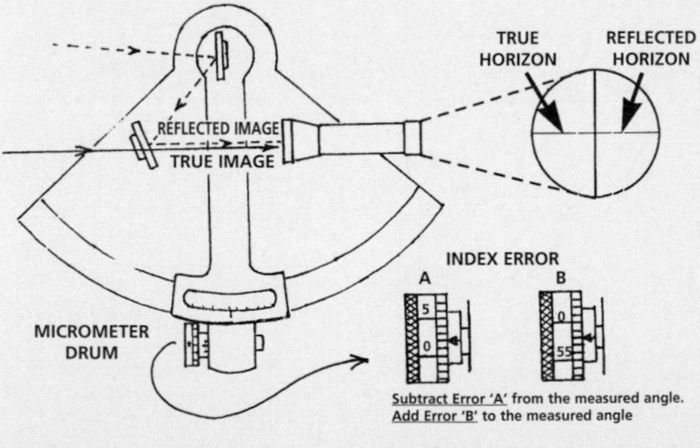

Distance off by vertical sextant angle

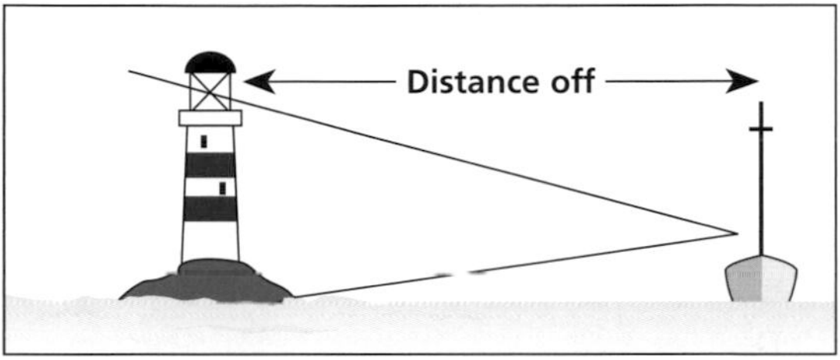

Vertical angle taken between the base of the lighthouse and* FOCAL PLANE *of the light,* NOT *the top of the lighthouse.

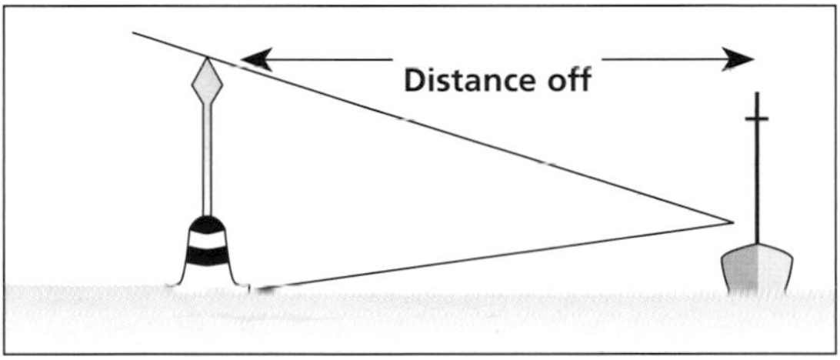

***Vertical angle taken between the base of the object and its* PEAK.**

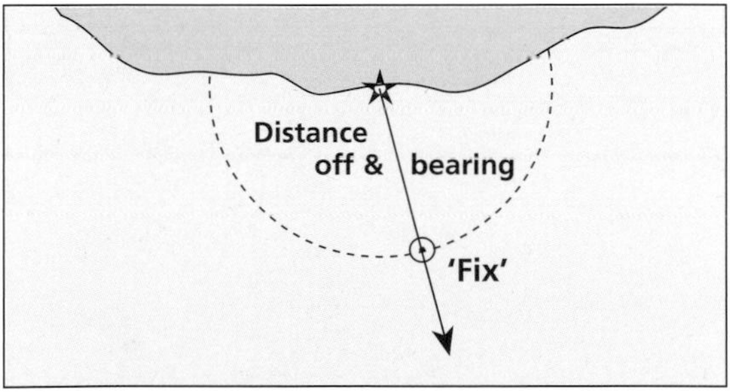

A bearing of the object and its distance off provide a 'fix'.

Vertical sextant angle

Taking a vertical sextant angle (VSA) on a lighthouse

Hold the sextant vertically, set the index to zero and view the centre of the light through the telescope. The true image will be seen through the plain half of the horizon glass and the reflected image in the mirror half (*Fig 1*).

Both images should coincide. Turn the micrometer drum so that the index bar moves along the arc away from you and the image will separate, the reflected image moving downward. Tilt the sextant to follow this movement until the centre of the light reaches the shore line. Read the angle and correct for index error (*Fig 2*).

Refer the corrected angle and the charted height of the light to the table on page 200 or to the appropriate table in the almanac to obtain a 'distance off'. Couple this with a bearing of the light taken at the same time as the sextant angle to obtain a 'fix' by bearing and distance.

Note

The height of an object on land is measured from the level of MHWS. If the sea level is below this datum when the sextant angle is taken, the apparent height of the object is increased, which also increases the angle being measured. This gives the impression that the boat is closer to the object than it actually is, and provides a slight safety margin. It should not be overlooked, however, that by the same reasoning, you will also be that much *closer* to any hazard that lies *behind* you.

Vertical sextant angle

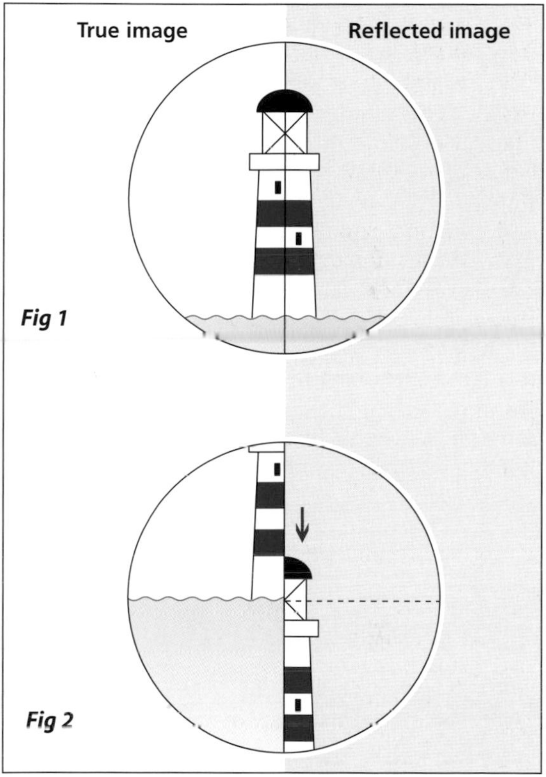

▸▸ Note

If an almanac or tables are unavailable, the distance off by vertical sextant angle can be found by using the formula:

$$\text{Distance off (nm)} = \frac{1.852 \times \text{height in metres}}{\text{angle in minutes of arc}}$$

Charted clearance

The clearance under a bridge or cable which crosses a navigable waterway is clearly marked on large scale charts of an area (Fig 1). The clearance hitherto has been measured from the level of MHWS but on some new editions of UKHO charts, the vertical clearance is now measured from the HAT level (see pages 28 & 29).

The water level under a bridge will seldom be as high as this so the clearance is usually greater than that given. It should be remembered however, that the water level in estuaries and rivers may be raised substantially by strong on-shore winds, heavy rainfall, or by the relief of weirs upstream; for these reasons a good margin for error should be allowed.

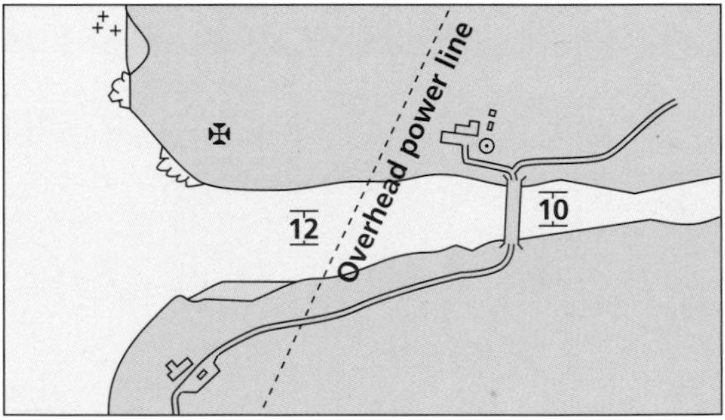

Fig 1

Caution

When you have made certain that your mast or the boat's superstructure will clear the bridge, be sure to check that at the same time you also have enough water below your keel.

Charted clearance

The difference between a *charted clearance* and the height of a vessel's mast (plus a suitable safety margin) is the fall of sea level below the given *clearance datum* that is needed to permit the vessel to pass under the bridge (*Fig 2*).

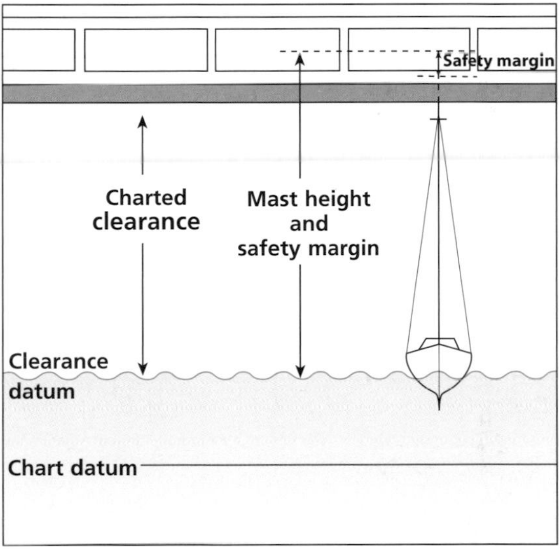

Fig 2 The appropriate clearance datum is given in the notes printed beneath all UKHO chart titles.

✱ Top tip

Whenever the height of your boat's mast or superstructure (plus safety margin) exceeds the charted clearance above the level of MHWS, you can use the tidal curves to find out when your boat will be able to pass under the bridge (see page 100).

Charted clearance – MHWS

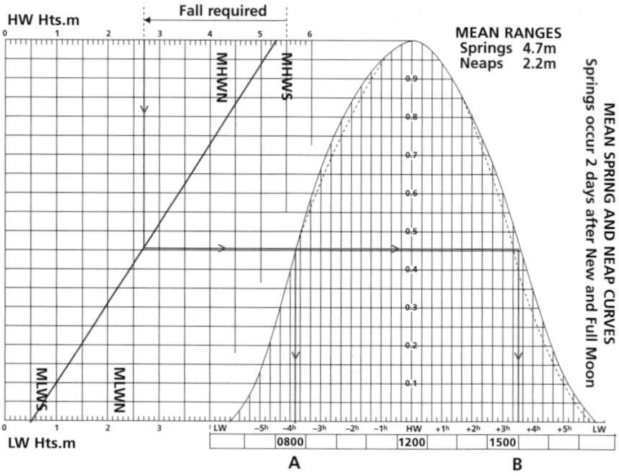

Devonport: mean spring and neap curves.

Using tidal curves to find clearance at MHWS

Mark up the appropriate curve with the day's tidal predictions (see page 70), then, starting from the MHWS level at the top of the graph, count off the fall required and from this point proceed as shown by the **red line** to find the time at which your boat will be able to pass under the bridge. In this example the boat will have clearance at any time earlier than **A** or later than **B**.

✱ Top tip

If the height of the tide indicated by the fall required is added to the charted depth near the bridge, you will also be able to determine whether or not you have sufficient water beneath your keel at the times that your mast will clear the bridge.

Key collision avoidance regulations

General conduct in any condition of visibility

- Maintain a proper lookout at all times.
- Adjust your speed to suit prevailing conditions.
- Know who should 'give way'.

Give-way vessel

- Take early, positive and obvious avoiding action.
- Do not cross ahead of the other vessel.

'Stand-on' vessel

- Hold a steady course and speed but be prepared to stop or turn away if the other vessel fails to take action.

Traffic separation schemes

Employed in congested areas and clearly marked on charts, they are 'one way' lanes for through traffic. Small boats and sailing craft should avoid them and use the Inshore Traffic Zones whenever possible or, if obliged to cross the lanes do so as quickly as possible on a ***heading at right angles*** to the general traffic flow. Vessels under 20 metres in length, and sailing vessels, must not impede the safe passage of power driven vessels following the lanes.

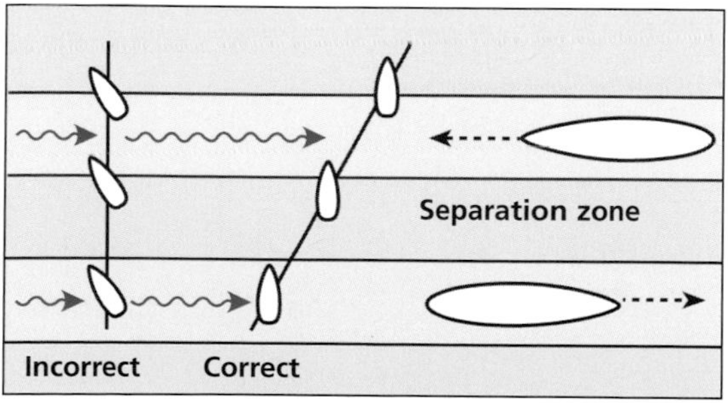

Steering and sailing rules

Collision avoidance (Rule 7)

When two vessels are steering in directions that would result in a collision if both maintained their courses and speeds, they are on collision courses and the 'give-way' vessel must take early avoiding action.

If you suspect that you are on a collision course with another vessel, take a bearing on it at regular intervals while maintaining your course and speed; and, in a situation similar to that shown, if the compass bearing becomes significantly smaller, the other vessel should pass ahead of you; if the bearings widen appreciably, it will pass astern, but if the bearing does not alter and the range is decreasing, one of you must take immediate action to avoid a collision.

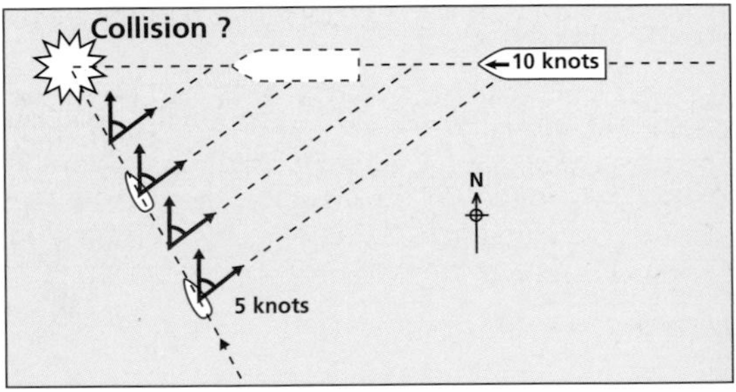

Note In a situation where the other vessel is on your port side, bearings will *increase* if it is to pass ahead of you and *decrease* for it to pass astern.

Caution

Risk of collision may sometimes still exist even with an appreciable change of bearing, for example, when you are approaching a very large vessel, particularly at close range.

Power-driven vessels – includes vessels sailing and using engines simultaneously

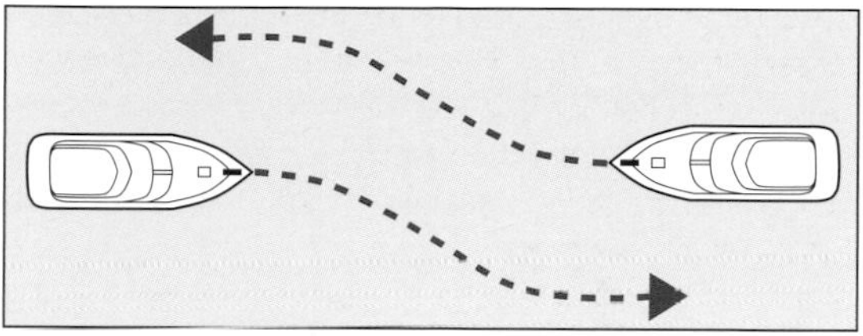

When meeting head on

- *Both* vessels turn to starboard.

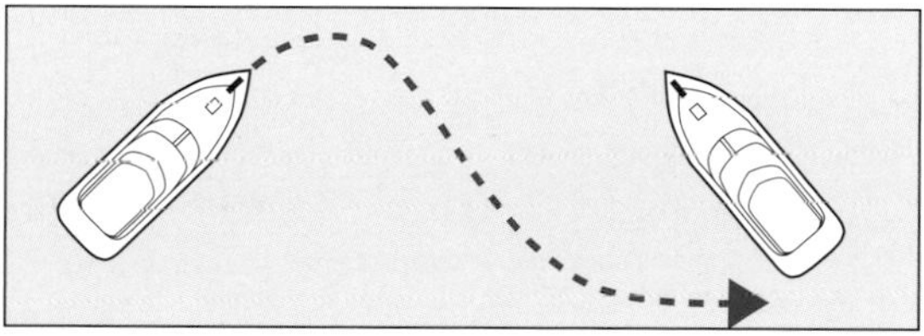

When crossing

- Vessel with another on her own starboard side gives way *and avoids crossing ahead*.

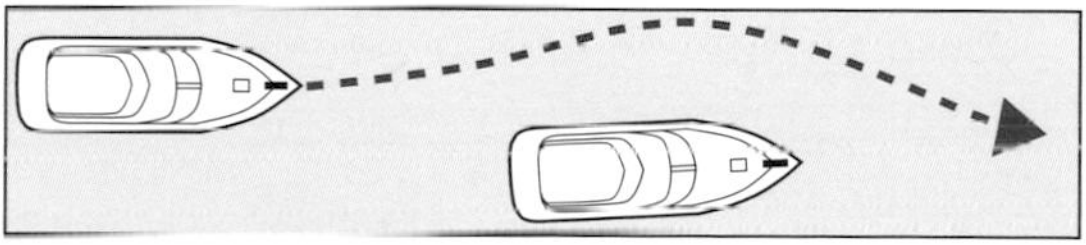

Overtaking vessel

Keeps clear of the vessel being overtaken.

Power-driven vessels keep clear of:

- Sailing vessels *not using power*.
- Vessels engaged in fishing.
- Vessels not under command (*unable to comply with the rules for some reason*).
- Vessels restricted in their ability to manoeuvre or hampered by their draught.

Steering and sailing rules

Sailing vessels meeting

A sailing vessel is on *port tack* when the wind is on its port side and the mainboom is out to starboard. It is on *starboard tack* when the wind comes from starboard and the mainboom is out to port.

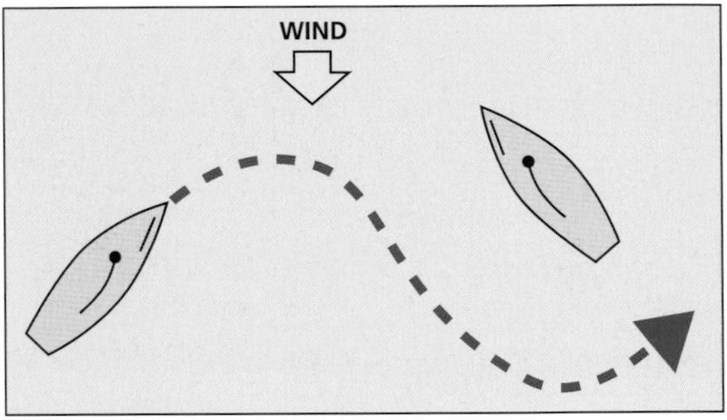

Vessels with wind on different sides. The vessel on port tack gives way.

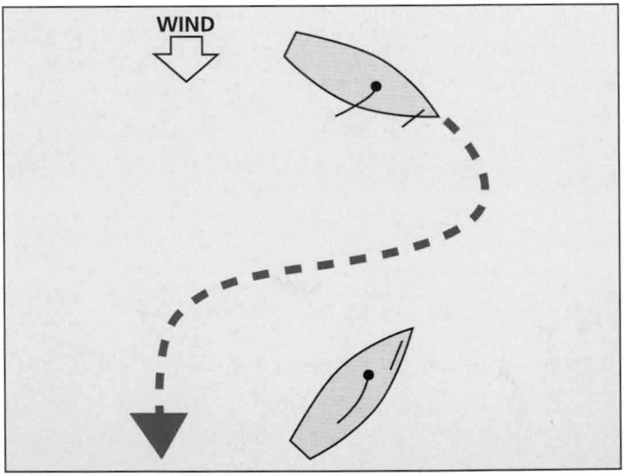

Vessels with wind on the same side. The windward boat gives way.

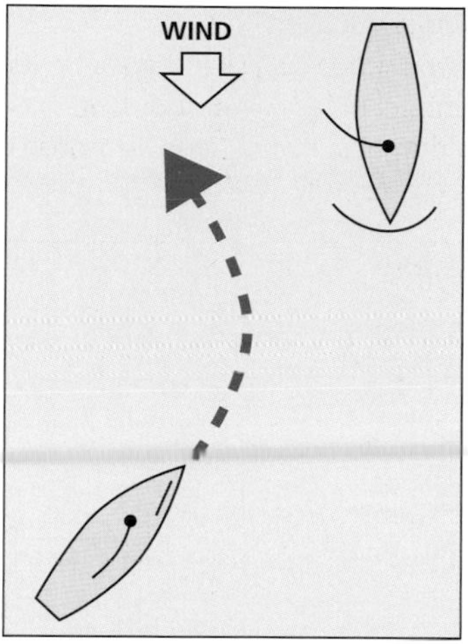

Sailing vessels meeting

A vessel with wind on her port side, that is unable to determine which tack a boat to windward of her is on, should prepare to give way.

Overtaking vessel

Keeps clear of the vessel being overtaken.

Sailing vessels (not using power) – keep clear of:

- Vessels engaged in fishing.
- Vessels not under command (*unable to comply with the rules*).
- Vessels restricted in their ability to manoeuvre or hampered by their draught.

Note

Sailing vessels using engines (with or without sails being set) are considered to be power-driven vessels and must conform to the steering and lighting regulations applicable to power-driven vessels.

Lights and daymarks on vessels

Definitions and arcs of visibility

Lights must be shown from sunset to sunrise and at all times during reduced visibility. Colours and cut off angles of lights are designed to indicate the type of vessel and direction of travel.

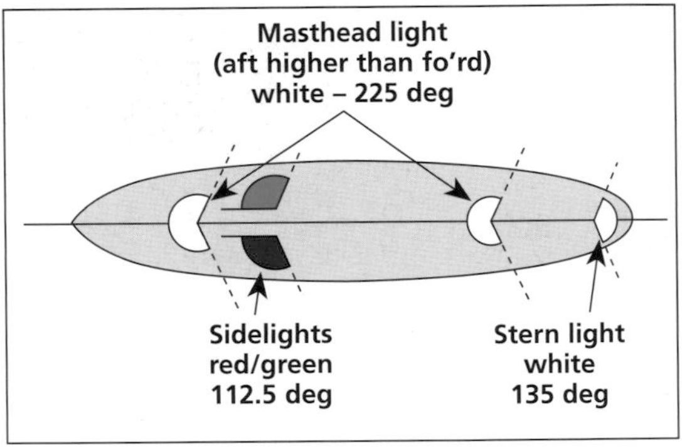

All round light

- Shows an unbroken light over an arc of 360° around the horizon.

Flashing light

- Regular flashes of 120 or more per minute (hydrofoils and air-cushion craft).

Towing light

- A yellow light with the same characteristics as a stern light and mounted above it.

Blue lights

- These are carried by Police and Customs vessels on duty.

Lights required for motor yachts

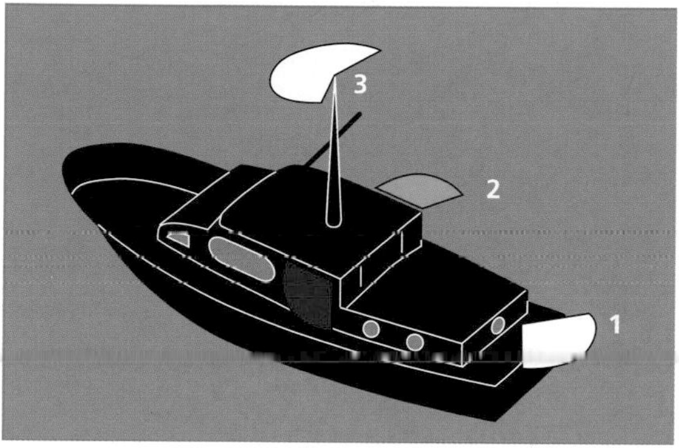

Vessels 12 to 20m LOA

1 A white stern light.
2 Red and green sidelights mounted separately or combined in a single bi-lantern.
3 A white masthead light shown at least 2·5m above the level of the sidelights.

Vessels under 12m LOA

- Must carry stern and side lights as specified above and a masthead light mounted a least 1m above the level of the side lights.
- The masthead light and stern light may be combined in a single lantern at or near the masthead.

Vessels under 7m LOA *maximum speed not exceeding 7kn*

- Required to carry a single all round white light but should also carry sidelights if practicable to do so.

Lights and daymarks on vessels

Sailing vessels under 20m

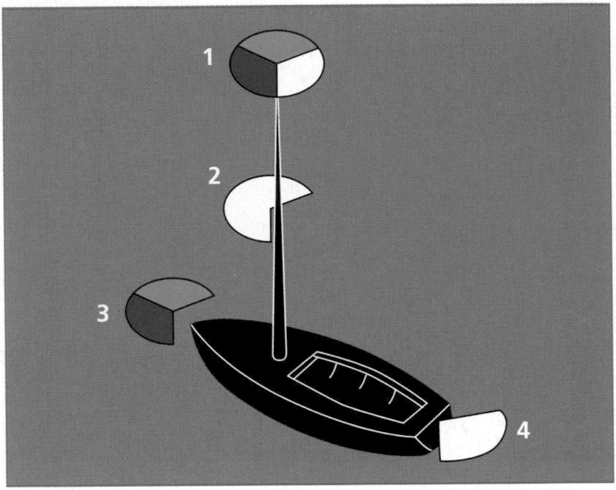

Sailing vessels not using power

- Show lanterns 1 **or** 3 and 4 in diagram above.
- Optional *all round* red over green masthead lights may also be shown with lanterns 3 and 4 but ***not*** in conjunction with lantern 1, or when using auxiliary power.

Sailing vessels using power

- Show lanterns 2, 3 and 4.
- Tri-lantern 1 must ***not*** be used when using auxiliary power.
- When using sail *and* power together by day, all vessels ***must*** exhibit a black cone point down in the fore-part where best seen.

Vessels under 7m in length

- If unable to exhibit these lights you ***must*** have a white light ready to display to avoid collision.

Hovercraft and hydrofoils

- Normal lights for power driven vessels and an all round flashing yellow light when in non-displacement mode.

Vessels towing

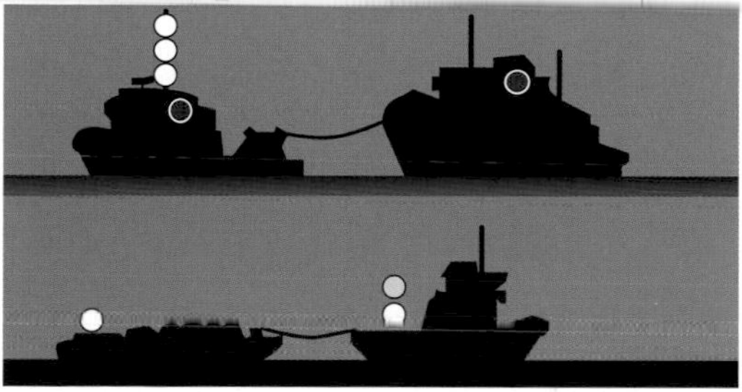

- Two masthead lights forward in a vertical line or if the length of tow exceeds 200m – three lights in a vertical line. Also side lights, stern light and a yellow light mounted above the stern light.

Vessel being towed

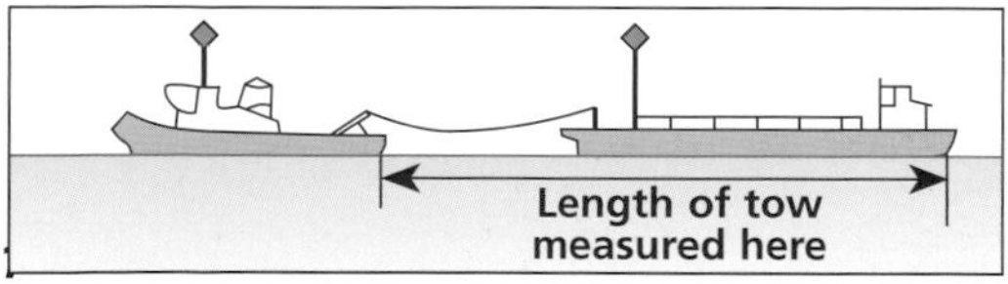

- Stern and sidelights only.

By day When length of tow is over 200m both vessels display a diamond shape.

Lights and daymarks on vessels

Vessel constrained by draught

- Three all round red lights with normal navigation lights when making way.

By day Shows a black cylinder.

Vessel not under command (unable to comply with the rules)

- Two all round red lights and when making way – stern and sidelights. (Not a distress signal.)

By day Shows two black balls in a vertical line.

Vessel aground

- Two all round red lights and anchor lights. (Not a distress signal.)

By day Shows three black balls in a vertical line.

Vessels trawling

- Two all round lights green over white and lights for a power driven vessel making way.

Pair trawling

- Vessels trawling as a pair direct searchlights forward and toward one another.

Vessel fishing (other than trawling)

- Two all round lights red over white plus stern and sidelights when making way.

By day Fishing or trawling: two cones apex together.

Additional signals – Vessels fishing in close proximity

Trawler hauling nets: ○ *Two all round lights* ●

Shooting nets: ○ *Two all round lights* ○

Vessel using purse seine gear: *Alternate flashing yellow* ○

Lights and daymarks on vessels

Vessels restricted in their ability to manoeuvre

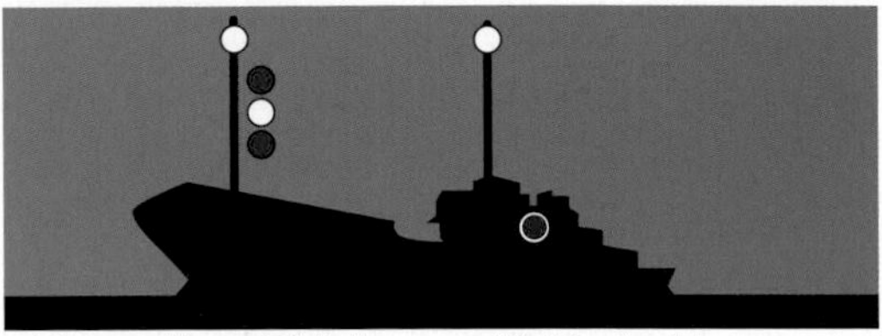

- Three all round lights – red/white/red in a vertical line and masthead – stern and sidelights when making way.

By day Shows a black ball over a diamond over a ball

Vessels engaged in underwater operations or dredging

- Two red lights in a vertical line on the 'foul side' and two green lights on the unobstructed side.
- When making way, also shows masthead, stern and sidelights. If anchored does ***not*** show anchor lights.

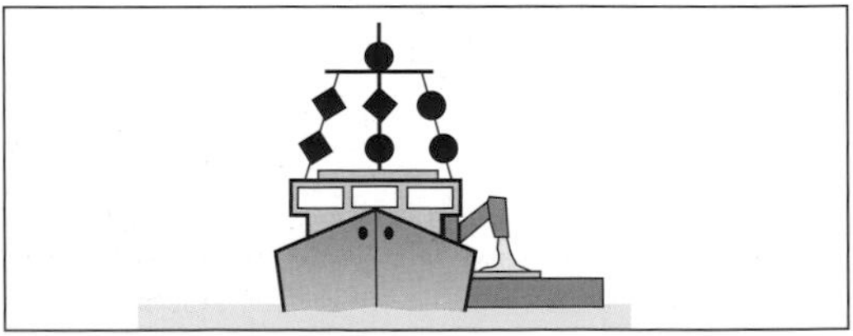

By day The red lights would be replaced by black balls and the green lights by black diamond shapes.

Vessels minesweeping

- Three all round green lights with normal navigation lights.

By day All round green lights are replaced by black balls.

★ **It is dangerous to approach closer than 1000m astern or 500m on either side of this vessel.**

Pilot vessel: on duty

- Two all round lights white over red and stern and sidelights when making way. At anchor shows an anchor light.

By day Flies a white and red flag.

Vessel at anchor

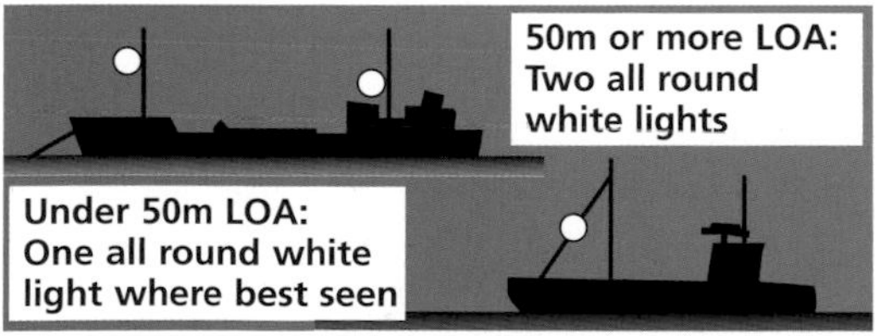

- Vessels more than 100m LOA must also illuminate their decks.

By day Shows a black ball.

Daymarks on vessels

Shapes of daymarks

Daymarks are displayed by day in various combinations and in all weathers to indicate certain activities in which the vessel carrying them is engaged.

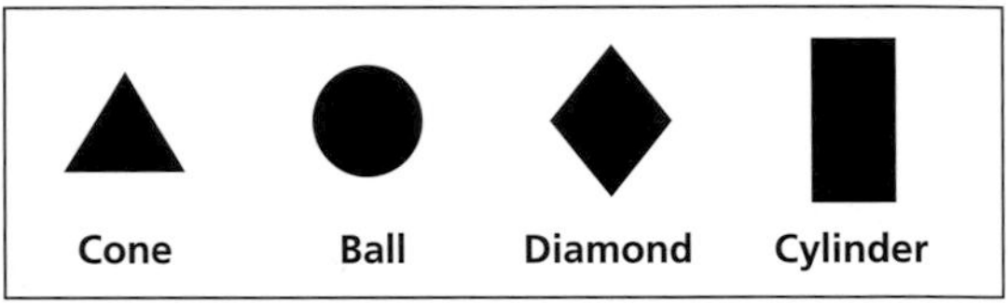

In conditions of reduced visibility, appropriate lights may also be shown.

Vessels under 20m in length engaged in fishing may exhibit a basket instead of the prescribed day shape for this type of vessel.

Survey vessels towing long seismic streamers mark the extremities of the tow with buoys flashing morse U ••— (international signal: 'you are running into danger').

A vessel engaged in diving operations that is too small to carry the day-shapes shown on page 112 ***must*** display a rigid replica of code Flag A:

Code flag A

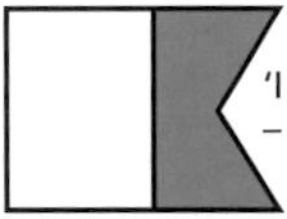

'I have a diver down –
– keep clear at low speed.'

Note

A vessel is deemed to be *underway* when not at anchor or moored to the shore and is *making way* when being propelled through the water by any means of propulsion.

Horn or whistle

Short blast ●　　　　Long blast ▬

Vessels in sight of each other – manoeuvring

◆ Turning to starboard	●
◆ Turning to port	● ●
◆ Engines in reverse	● ● ●
◆ Alert 'wake up'	● ● ● ● ●

Vessel in narrow channel

◆ Nearing blind bends	▬
◆ Intent to overtake:	
to starboard	▬ ▬ ●
to port	▬ ▬ ● ●
◆ Agreement by other vessel	▬ ● ▬ ●

During poor visibility (day or night)

Sounded at two minute intervals

◆ Power vessel making way	▬
◆ Under way but ***not*** making way (See note page 114)	▬ ▬
◆ Not under command ◆ Unable to manoeuvre ◆ Hampered by draught ◆ Vessel fishing ◆ Vessel towing/pushing ◆ Sailing vessel (not using power)	▬ ● ●
◆ Vessel under tow (If manned)	▬ ● ● ●

Sound signals

Vessels at anchor or aground (in poor visibility)

At anchor

- Vessels under 100m in length must ring a bell for 5 sec every minute.
- A vessel 100m or more in length must ring a bell 'forward' for 5 sec every minute immediately followed by a gong sounded for 5 sec 'aft'.
- Any vessel at anchor may also give a warning of collision to an approaching vessel by sounding morse 'R' (• — •) on a horn.

Vessels aground

- Signals as for at anchor but preceded and followed by 3 separate and distinct bell strokes.

Vessels under 12m in length

- May make the appropriate sound signals given above or ***must*** make some other efficient sound signal at intervals of not less than 2 min.

Important note

This abridged interpretation of parts A, B, C and D of the rules must only be read and used in conjunction with the full rules given in the International Regulations for Preventing Collision at Sea (IRPCS). The rules are mandatory and there is no excuse for not knowing them. Rules 1 and 2 stipulate: 'These rules shall apply to all vessels upon the high seas and in all waters connected therewith navigable by sea going vessels' and 'nothing in the rules shall exonerate any vessel or the owner, master or crew thereof from the consequences of any neglect to comply with these rules'.

IALA Maritime Buoyage System

Lateral marks Used in the conventional direction of buoyage to define the limits of navigable channels in the general direction of harbour from seaward.

The symbol: 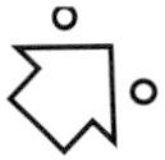

is used on charts to show the direction of buoyage where this is not obvious.

Preferred channel marks Modified lateral marks are used to mark the point where a channel divides when proceeding in the conventional direction of buoyage and to indicate the main or preferred channel.

Isolated danger mark Used to indicate an isolated danger of limited size which has navigable water all around it.

Safe water mark Used as a centre channel or landfall mark with deep navigable water all around it.

Cardinal marks These cover the four quadrants: N, S, E and W. Each mark is named after the quadrant it guards and indicates the side upon which it should be passed in safety, ie pass to the north of a north cardinal.

Special marks These can be any shape and are used to mark areas of particular interest such as spoil grounds, water sport or military exercise areas etc.

New wreck marking buoy Deployed until a wreck is well known and has been promulgated in nautical publications and a permanent form of marking has been established.

Buoys and marks

Cardinal marks

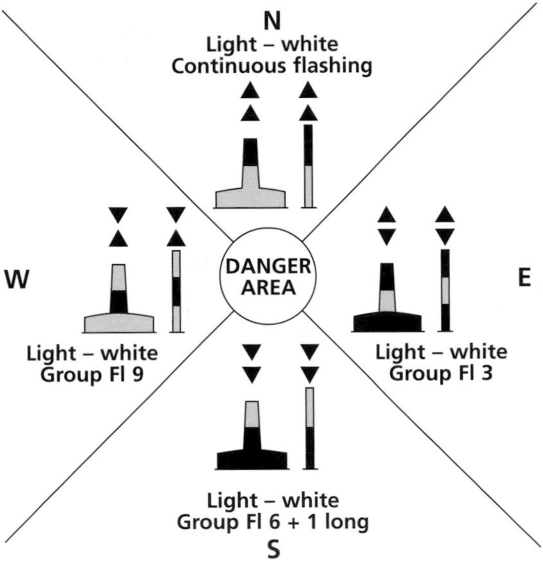

Isolated danger mark

Danger with safe water all round
Light – white Group Fl 2

Safe water mark

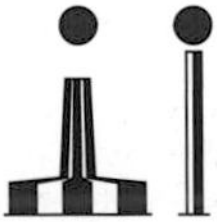

Safe deep water all round
Light – white. Occulting, isophase, or 1 long flash or Morse 'A'
Pass either side, but leave to port when entering or leaving a channel entrance

Buoys and marks

Lateral marks – region 'A'

Port hand
red can

Starboard hand
green cone

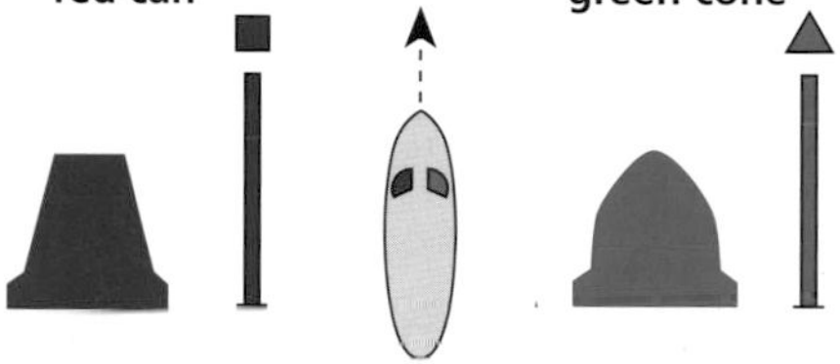

Light – red
any rhythm except
composite Gp Fl 2+1

Light – green
any rhythm except
composite Gp Fl 2+1

Preferred channel marks (modified lateral marks)

Main channel
to the right

Main channel
to the left

Direction of
buoyage

Light – composite
Gp Fl 2 + 1 red

Light – composite
Gp Fl 2 +1 green

Special Marks

(any shape – yellow

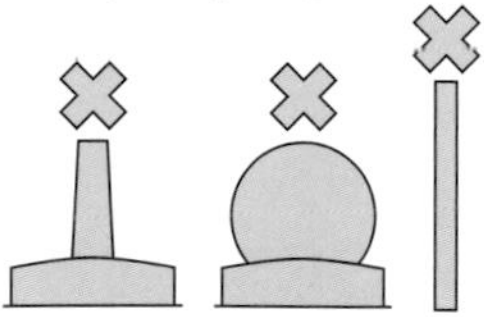

Yellow Light (if lit) any rhythm other than those prescribed for cardinal, isolated danger or safe water marks.

'New Hazard' Mark

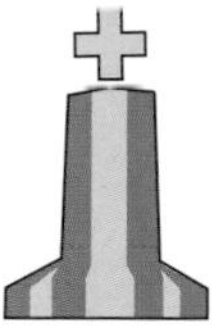

Light – Alt. Blue/Yellow

Emergency Wreck Marking Buoy – deployed in the initial period following a wreckage

Light characteristics

Light characteristics	*Int abbr*	*Period shown*
Fixed *A continuous steady light*	**F**	
Occulting *Steady light – eclipsed at regular and repeated intervals*		
Single	**Oc**	
Group	**Oc (2)**	
Isophase *Duration – light and dark equal*	**Iso**	
Flashing *Single flashes at regular intervals. Duration of light less than dark*		
Single	**Fl**	
Long	**L Fl**	
Group	**Fl (3)**	
Composite group	**Fl (2+1)**	
Morse code	**Mo (K)**	
Alternating *Light which alters colour in successive flashes*	**Al WR**	

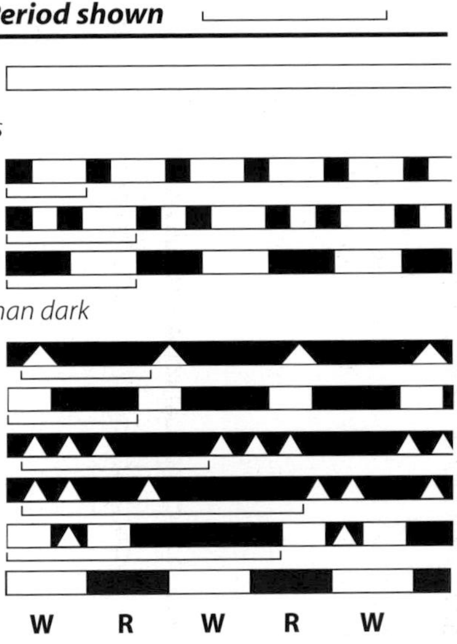

Sectored light *Shows different colour light when viewed from different directions*

Safety Of Life At Sea (SOLAS)

Sailors who fail to comply with the SOLAS regulations, mandatory for all leisure craft users from 1 July 2002, risk prosecution and fines of up to £5000. Also, in instances where it is proved that fatalities have occurred because of non-compliance, a jail sentence could be imposed.

Mandatory regulations – SOLAS chapter V

19 Radar reflectors If it is 'practicable' to fit one on your boat then you ***must*** have one.

29 Life saving signals An illustrated diagram depicting these signals must be readily available on board (see pages 128–9).

31–32 Danger messages All skippers have a duty to report to the Coastguard anything that might be a serious hazard to navigation.

33 Distress signals Skippers have an obligation to respond to distress signals from any source and to assist as best they can.

34 Safe navigation and avoidance of danger
(See page 122 Passage Planning.)

35 Distress signals – misuse The use of a signal for anything other than an emergency is prohibited.

✷ Top tip
As far as possible, always avoid any action or activity that might be harmful to the environment (Rule 2.4).

Passage planning

Passage planning (Reg V.34)

Skippers who take their boats 'to sea', which means anywhere outside *categorised waters*, ***must*** have a passage plan. For small vessels and leisure craft, the extent of the plan depends upon the vessel's size and the length of the voyage but consideration should be given to:

The limitations of the boat

- Is it a suitable boat in which to make the proposed passage.
- Does it carry appropriate safety equipment and have sufficient fuel, water and provisions.

Crew strength

- The competence, experience and physical ability of both skipper and crew.

Tides

- Check tidal predictions in order to make best use of favourable tidal streams and heights of tide.

Weather

- Check the forecast before departure and obtain regular updates en-route.

Contingency plans

- Tell someone ashore where you are going.
- Have a plan of action in case things go wrong.
- Make a note of 'ports of refuge' en-route.

Caution

Don't rely solely on GPS. Plot your course and regularly record your position on the chart.

Emergencies – calling for help using flares

Red flares and orange smoke These are used to attract attention in case of difficulty and to pinpoint your position for searching rescue craft.

White flares ***These are not distress signals*** – they are only used to warn others of danger of collision.

Types of distress flare

There are three main types of distress flare, all with different ignition systems. Read the instructions and familiarise yourself with each type of flare before you need to use them in an emergency and ensure that they are in-date – old flares become very unreliable.

- **Hand-held red** Use day or night when near to the shore or to assist rescue craft to see you. Wear gloves if possible, hold at arm's length downwind and don't look directly at the flare.
- **Orange smoke** These are hand-held or buoyant types. Useful to help rescue helicopters identify your position and to assess wind direction.
- **Red parachute rocket** Can be seen for up to 25 miles in good visibility. It rises to about 300 metres then falls slowly under the parachute. Fire vertically or slightly downwind or in low cloud, fire at 45°. **Never fire a parachute flare if a helicopter is approaching.**

✷ Top tip

Fire flares in groups of two – they are more likely to be seen than singly. Hold flares downwind and outboard so that any burning dross falls clear of the boat.

GMDSS/EPIRB

Emergencies – calling for help

Red flares and *VHF radio* have long been the mariner's principal means of signalling distress but now, the *Global Maritime Distress and Safety Scheme (GMDSS)* and a radio equipped with *Digital Selective Calling (DSC)* will enable you to send or receive distress and safety messages quicker than ever before.

In an emergency, a coded *distress alert*, which includes the vessel's unique identity number and its current position, is automatically transmitted on CH 70 when a dedicated button on the radio set is pressed. This signal is repeated at short intervals until a *distress acknowledgement* sent by a ship or shore station automatically stops the distress transmission and retunes the radio to CH 16 ready for voice communication.

Yachtsmen are not obliged to convert to DSC; you can still use your existing *VHF radio* to call other yachts and the UK Coastguard who will continue to monitor CH 16 until the year 2005 but you will need DSC to call ships, who are not now obliged to maintain a listening watch on CH 16, and by 2005, in most parts of Europe, coastguards and coast radio stations will only be keeping a watch on CH 70 so you will need VHF/DSC to be able to call them.

If you intend sailing more than a mile or two off shore, you should also carry an *Emergency Position Indicating Radio Beacon (EPIRB)*.

✱ Top tip

False alerts are a big problem with EPIRBS. If you need to remove yours from the boat – for service or repair for instance – ensure that it is double wrapped in aluminium foil to prevent accidental radiation of signals.

Distress or emergency signals (VHF)

These are only to be used when there is grave and imminent danger to a vessel or person and immediate assistance is required.

Switch on the radio – select channel 16
Transmit on high power

1. **Mayday – Mayday – Mayday**
2. **This is** – Name of vessel three times
3. **Mayday** – Name of vessel once
4. **Give your position**
5. **State the nature of the emergency**
6. **Type of assistance required**
7. **Give any other helpful information**
8. **Over** – end of message

If the emergency does not warrant a full Mayday alert (or if in doubt) the *URGENCY* call may be used instead:

1. **PanPan – PanPan – PanPan**
2. **All stations – All stations – All stations**
3. **This is** – Name of vessel three times
4. **Give your position**
5. **State the nature of the emergency**
6. **Type of assistance required**
7. **Over** – end of message

Other recognised signals for help are: *SOS* in Morse code by light or sound. *Letters NC* by flag or Morse code. *A ball shape* displayed over or under a *square shape*. Continuous sounding of *fog horn*.

Personal safety

Hypothermia One of the greatest dangers to sailors is the cold so always try to stay warm and dry by wearing suitable clothing whatever the weather. In water the human body loses heat 25 times faster than in air and without special clothing, you are unlikely to survive in water of 10°C for longer than four hours.

Lifejackets These must be available for *all* the crew. Lifejacket buoyancy is measured in newtons. Ten newtons equal 1kg of flotation and a 150N jacket is the standard recommended for offshore yachts and motor cruisers. When inflated, this jacket will right an unconscious body and lift the mouth and nose above the water. Lifejackets should be worn at all times by children and non swimmers, also by anyone leaving the safety of the cockpit at night or in rough weather and – ***routinely when going ashore in the dinghy***.

Harness At night and in rough weather, everyone on deck should wear a safety harness clipped on to a dedicated strong point on the boat – ***not to the guard rails***. Adjust the harness to fit snugly over your oilskins so that it is easy to put on – even in the dark.

Liferafts The number of crew on the boat should not exceed the capacity of the liferaft. Have it serviced annually and stow it in a position ready for immediate use with its painter (release cord) tied on and ***any anti-theft device removed***.

Abandoning to the liferaft ***Do not abandon unless the boat is on fire or you are certain that it will sink or be wrecked***. Check that the painter is tied on, throw the raft to leeward and tug the painter to inflate it. Let the strongest and heaviest crewmember climb in first to stabilise the raft and to help others to board.

Hi-line transfer

- Downdraught from the helicopter will be very strong so ensure that all loose gear on the deck is secured or stowed away before the helicopter arrives.
- Use **red hand-held flares** or **orange smoke** to signal your position if necessary. **Do not fire parachute flares when the helicopter is close by**.
- Once VHF contact has been established, the helicopter pilot will give you instructions and outline his intentions before he reaches you. Make sure that you understand them, it will be too noisy to hear your radio once the helicopter is overhead. **Closely follow any instructions you are given**.
- The helmsman should try to maintain a steady course – usually with the wind 30° on the port bow to enable the helicopter pilot to stay head to wind while winching from his starboard side.
- When the helicopter is in position, a weighted line will be lowered first. Allow it to touch the boat or the water to discharge any static electricity then take up the slack and stow the loose end in a bucket to avoid snagging. **Do not tie the line to the boat**.
- As the winchman is lowered on the wire, keep some tension on the line but only pull it in when told to do so – this may require the efforts of two people. Once the winchman is safely aboard, obey his instructions and let him look after the casualty.
- When the winchman and the casualty are being lifted off, keep enough tension on the line to prevent swinging and do not cast the hi-line clear until told to do so.

Calling for help – Life saving signals

Signals to be used by ships, aircraft, or persons in distress when communicating with life-saving stations, maritime rescue units and aircraft engaged in search and rescue operations

Search and Rescue Unit Replies

You have been seen, assistance will be given as soon as possible.

Orange smoke flare.

OR

Three white star signals or three light and sound rockets fired at approximately 1 minute intervals.

Surface to Air Signals

Message	International Code of signals			ICAO/IMO Visual Signals
Require assistance	V		• • • —	V
Require medical assistance	W		• — —	X
No or negative	N		— •	N
Yes or affirmative	C		— • — •	Y
Proceeding in this direction				↑

Note: Use International Code of Signals by means of lights or flags or by laying out the symbol on the deck or ground with items which contrast highly with the background.

Air to Surface Direction Signals

Sequence of 3 manoeuvres meaning proceed to this direction.

1

Circle vessel at least once.

2

Cross low, ahead of vessel rocking wings.

3

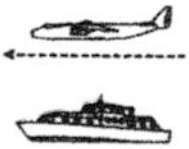

Overfly vessel and head in required direction.

Your assistance is no longer required

Cross low, astern of vessel rocking wings.

Note: As a non preferred alternative to rocking wings, varying engine tone or volume may be used.

hore to Ship Signals

afe to land here.

OR

— • —

K

Morse code signal by light or sound

rtical waving of both arms, white flag, light or flare.

nding here is dangerous. Additional signals mean safer landing in rection indicated.

OR

S: • • •

Morse code signals by light or sound.

R: • — •

Land to the right of your current heading.

L: • — • •

Land to the left of your current heading.

rizontal waving of white flag, light or flare. tting one flag, light or flare on ground and oving off with a second indicates direction of fer landing.

r to Surface Replies

essage Understood.

OR OR OR

— OR • — •

T R

op a message | Rocking wings. | Flashing landing or navigation lights on and off twice. | Morse code signal by light.

essage Not Understood – Repeat.

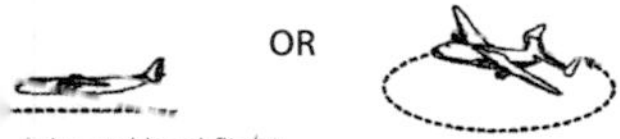

OR OR

• — •   • — — •   —

R P T

aight and level flight | Circling. | Morse code signal by light.

rface to Air Replies

essage Understood – I will comply.

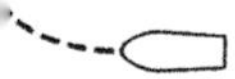

Change course required direction.

OR

—

T

Morse code signal by light.

OR

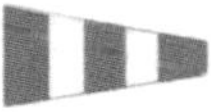

Code & answering pendant 'Close Up'

m unable to comply.

te: Use the signal st appropriate to vailing conditions.

— •

N

Morse code signal by light.

OR

International Flag 'N'

Man overboard

Prevention

In rough weather or at night, wear suitable protective clothing and a lifejacket fitted with reflective tape, a whistle and a light. Non-swimmers and children should wear a lifejacket at all times when on deck. Use a correctly fitting harness clipped on to a secure attachment point – ***not onto the guard rails***. Jackstays rigged along each side of the boat will enable you to walk the full length of the deck without unclipping. Always try to 'clip on short' so that if you do slip, you will fall on to the deck and not over the side.

First reactions

Immediately shout 'Man overboard' and drop the horseshoe and danbuoy into the water. Detail someone to watch and point towards the casualty. Hit the MOB function button on the electronic 'navaid' if one is in use, to record where the person fell overboard. If you lose sight of the person in the water or have any doubts about your ability to recover him, ***do not delay, put out a Mayday call on your VHF radio*** (page 125).

MOB recovery drill

The two generally accepted methods of returning to a person overboard are the 'reach, tack, reach' method or the 'quick stop' method. For any given emergency, the most suitable procedure will always depend to a large extent upon prevailing conditions, type of boat and crew size. Practice recovery drill regularly, and under different conditions if possible. One day someone's life may depend on it!

Getting someone back on board can be difficult. Always tie him to the boat first before trying to get him aboard and clip yourself on too so that you cannot be pulled in on top of him.

A boarding ladder or a short rope with a bowline as a foot loop can be used if the person in the water is able to help. If they are unconscious or exhausted, some form of lifting tackle will have to be rigged up. For example: swing out the boom guyed fore and aft and use the mainsheet to winch the casualty onboard. If another crew member has to enter the water to help the casualty, ***he MUST wear a lifejacket and be attached to the boat by a strong line***.

Person in the water

Try not to panic and do not try to swim after the boat. Look for the lifebuoy which should be close by. The greatest threat to your survival is from the cold so try to conserve body heat by restricting your movements. Cross your legs to keep them close together and pull your knees up towards your chest. Turn your back to the waves to keep your nose and mouth clear of the spray.

Note

Research has established that when a MOB is lifted from the water vertically, blood sinks to the legs lowering blood pressure, and this might result in a heart attack. Recovery using a cradle, or something similar to keep the casualty horizontal is safer, especially if the person is unconscious.

MOB – sailing boat without engine

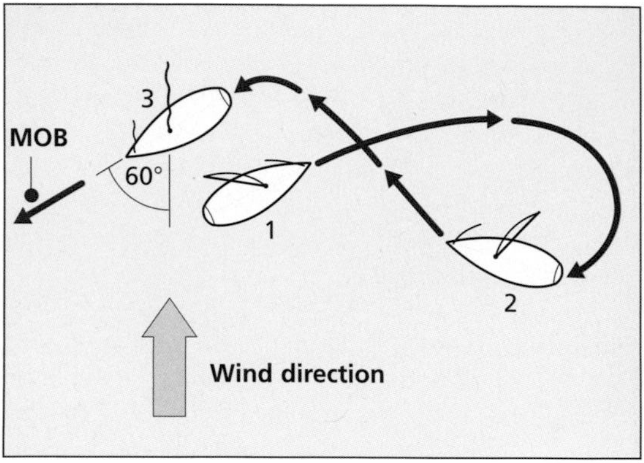

MOB – Sailing boat without engine

1 Put the boat on to a beam reach for a few boat lengths.

2 Tack on to the opposite beam reach to bring the person in the water on the weather bow.

3 When down wind of the casualty, tack again, ease the sheets and fore-reach to approach and come alongside to windward of the person in the water and make the recovery in the lee of the boat.

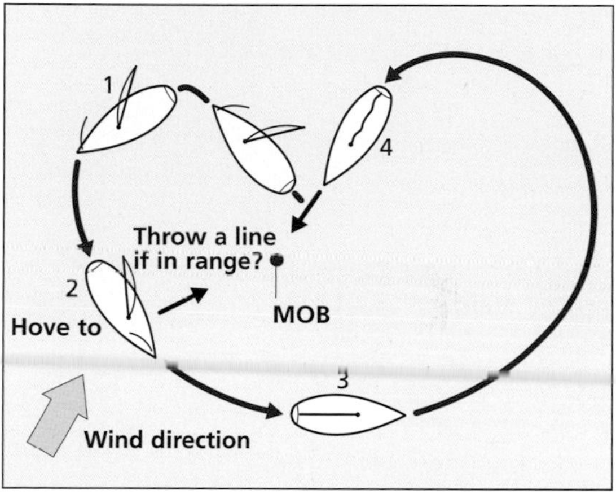

MOB – (quick stop) –sailing boat using engine

1 Come up into wind immediately and tack but leave the headsail cleated so that the boat stops hove to.

2 Throw a heaving line to the person in the water if you are still close enough; if not, check for trailing lines in the water and start the engine. Haul the mainsheet in tight and furl the headsail.

3 Motor down wind to leeward of the person in the water.

4 Turn to approach him head to wind with your mainsail flapping amidships.

> **▶▶ Caution**
> Ensure that the propeller is not turning once you are alongside the person in the water.

MOB – motor cruisers

Make a tight 180° U turn if you can clearly see the person in the water, if not, the 'Williamson Turn' is a good way to put your boat onto a reciprocal course:

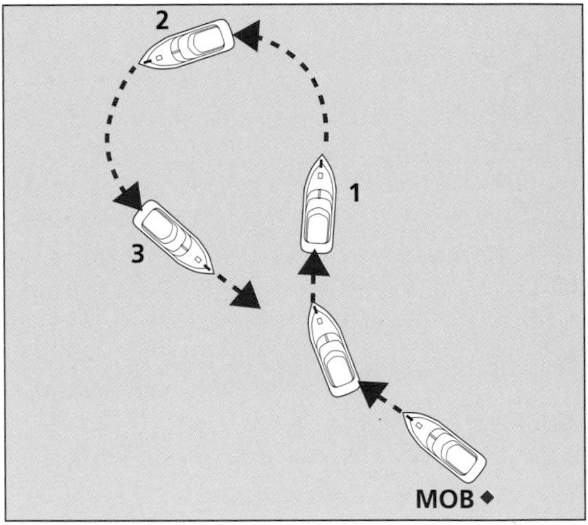

1 Put the helm hard over to starboard until you have added about 50° to your heading (this angle will vary from boat to boat) then:

2 Spin the wheel onto the opposite lock and hold it there slowing as you turn until you are moving back along your original track (**3**). The casualty should be somewhere ahead of you but remember that he/she will have drifted with the tide.

> **Caution**
> Ensure that your propellers are not turning when you draw close to the person in the water.

Words and Morse

A	ALPHA	• —	**N**	NOVEMBER	— •
B	BRAVO	— • • •	**O**	OSCAR	— — —
C	CHARLIE	— • — •	**P**	PAPA	• — — •
D	DELTA	— • •	**Q**	QUEBEC	— — • —
E	ECHO	•	**R**	ROMEO	• — •
F	FOXTROT	• • — •	**S**	SIERRA	• • •
G	GOLF	— — •	**T**	TANGO	—
H	HOTEL	• • • •	**U**	UNIFORM	• • —
I	INDIA	• •	**V**	VICTOR	• • • —
J	JULIET	• — — —	**W**	WHISKEY	• — —
K	KILO	— • —	**X**	X-RAY	— • • —
L	LIMA	• — • •	**Y**	YANKEE	— • — —
M	MIKE	— —	**Z**	ZULU	— — • •

Numbers and Morse

0 NADA-ZERO	— — — — —	**5** PANTA-FIVE	• • • • •
1 UNA-ONE	• — — — —	**6** SOXI-SIX	— • • • •
2 BISSO-TWO	• • — — —	**7** SETTE-SEVEN	— — • • •
3 TERRA-THREE	• • • — —	**8** OKTO-EIGHT	— — — • •
4 KARTA-FOUR	• • • • —	**9** NOVE-NINE	— — — — •

Morse code is no longer used to send messages but it should not be neglected by the sailor because S O S • • • — — — • • • by morse is internationally recognized as a distress signal and, of course, many charted buoys and beacons have lights with morse characteristcs ie:

Safe water mark Mo 'A' (• —)

Lighted offshore platform Mo 'U' (• • —)

Fog signal – siren Mo 'N' (— •)

Flags

International code of signals

Communication between vessels nowadays is usually carried out by radio, but code signals may also be sent by flag, light, or sound.

Single letter signals are perhaps the most important code signals and are understood internationally. Each letter of the alphabet except R is a complete message when sent individually, for example:

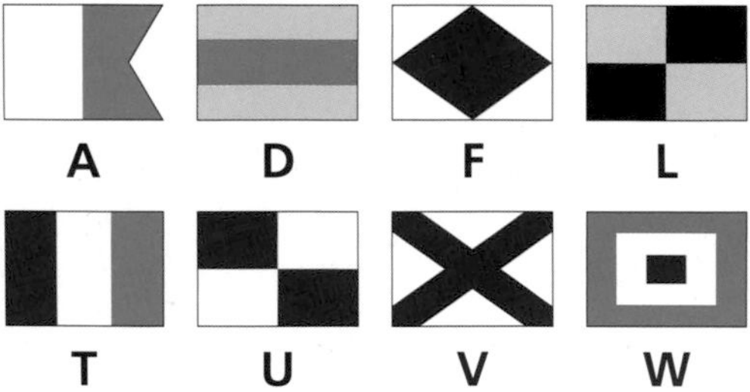

A I have a diver down. Keep clear.

D Keep clear. Manoeuvring with difficulty.

F I am disabled. Communicate with me.

L You should stop your vessel instantly.

T Keep clear – Pair trawling.

U You are running into danger.

V I require assistance.

W I require medical assistance.

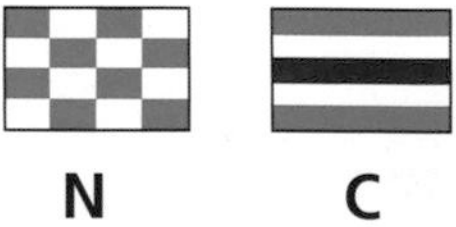

Flags N and C displayed together signify **distress**

Racing – code flags

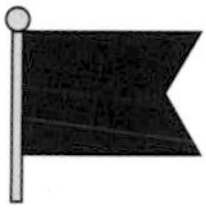

Protest

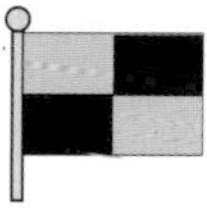

Come within hail

Mark missing

Abandoned

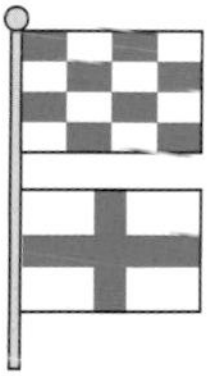

Abandoned Resail shortly

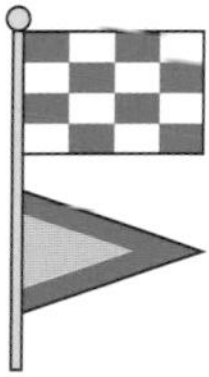

Cancellation

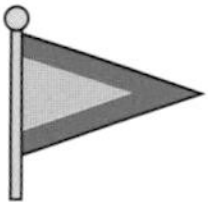

General recall

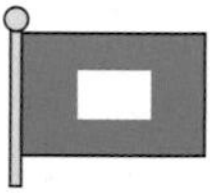

Preparatory

Life belts compulsory

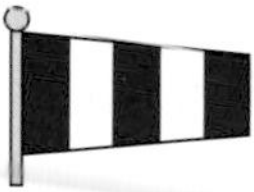

Postponement

15 minute postponement (*Black ball hoisted*)

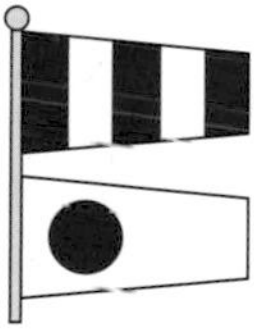

One hour postponement

Two hour postponement

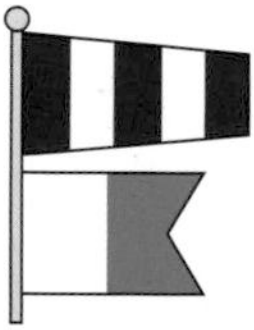

Postponement until a later date

The meaning of single letter code flags when used for racing purposes

Weather patterns – a summary

Causes of weather patterns

Variations in weather conditions are the direct result of changes in temperature within the moist dense air mass that envelops the Earth. The air exerts a pressure on the surface of the Earth and atmospheric pressure at sea level, measured by barometer, averages 1013·2mb, but radiant energy from the sun heats the surface unevenly so that the atmosphere is warmer in some places than in others; since warm air is less dense than cold air it rises – cold air sinks to replace it – and variations above and below average pressure occur resulting in regions of relatively high and low pressure.

Air always moves from a region of high pressure to one of lower pressure – but not directly because the movement is deflected by the rotation of the Earth. The flow of air is felt as wind whenever there is a difference in atmospheric pressure between two localities; its strength is determined by the rate of change in pressure between the two centres.

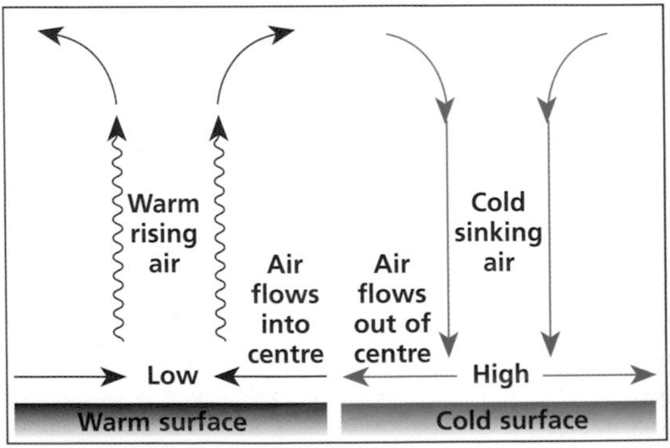

Wind belts

This global convection process results in a pattern of pressure and wind belts around the Earth but there are also local patterns.

Generally, when air is moving down in an area of high pressure, the weather is dry and settled, but where the air is rising and pressure is low the weather is disturbed because rising air cools, expands and condenses into cloud and this rising air draws in more of the surrounding air masses to fuel the process.

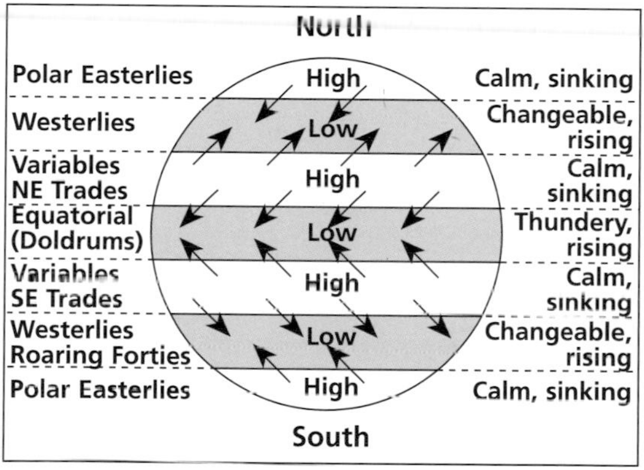

General circulation of the rotating Earth's atmosphere.

Barometric pressure

Variation in barometric pressure is one of the sailor's principle indications of impending changes to wind and weather in his area.

In general, barometer steady, or rising steadily indicates fair weather. Falling slowly indicates rain – possibly wind. Falling or rising rapidly indicates strong wind – probably rain.

Anticyclones and depressions

Highs and lows

Anticyclones and *depressions* (highs and lows) are the two main weather systems of the middle latitudes. In the northern hemisphere, an anticyclone is a system where winds blow in a clockwise direction around areas of high pressure. The strongest winds blow round the outer extremities of the area and gradually diminish in strength toward the centre where they are light or non-existent.

Anticyclones are fair weather systems with moderate winds and reasonably clear skies. They are generally slow moving, sometimes remaining stationary for several days.

Depressions and their associated fronts are largely responsible for unsettled weather, strong winds and heavy rainfall. A depression is an area of low pressure around which the winds blow in an anti-clockwise direction in the northern hemisphere. They vary greatly in size and intensity and can move rapidly in any direction but most usually eastward.

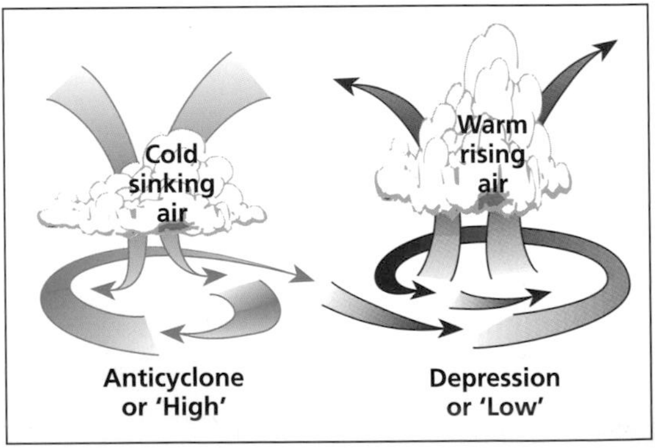

Weather fronts

A 'front' is the boundary between two kinds of air. The main air masses which affect British waters originate from either the Polar or sub-tropical highs. Although classified according to its source, each air mass may arrive by different routes, therefore its properties will depend upon its path and the general kind of weather to be expected from each mass is:

- *Arctic and Polar* – cold
- *Tropical* – warm
- *Maritime* – wet
- *Continental* – dry

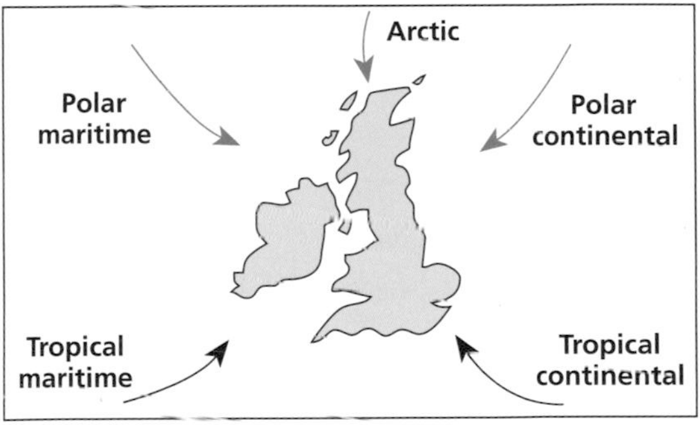

Most depressions that approach Britain form along the Polar front – the name given to the boundary between these two air masses.

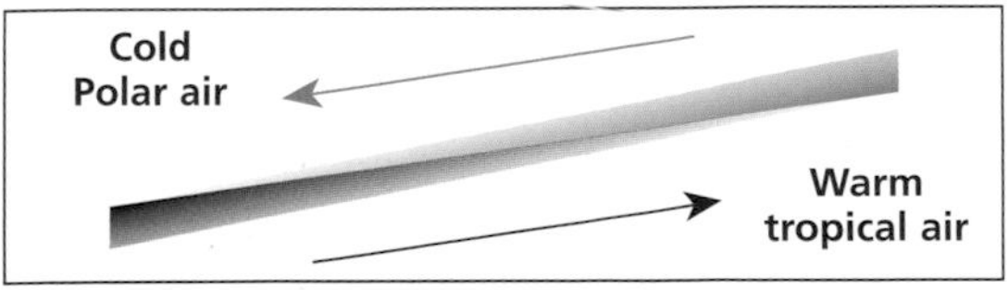

Front with opposing air currents.

Depressions

How depressions develop

When warm and cold air masses meet they interact and a wave develops in the front with its tip on the pole-ward side. Atmospheric pressure at the tip of the wave commences to fall until a complete circulation of air around a low pressure centre is established and a sector of warm air has become trapped in a squeeze between the cold air behind and the cool air ahead producing the fronts which are characteristic of a depression.

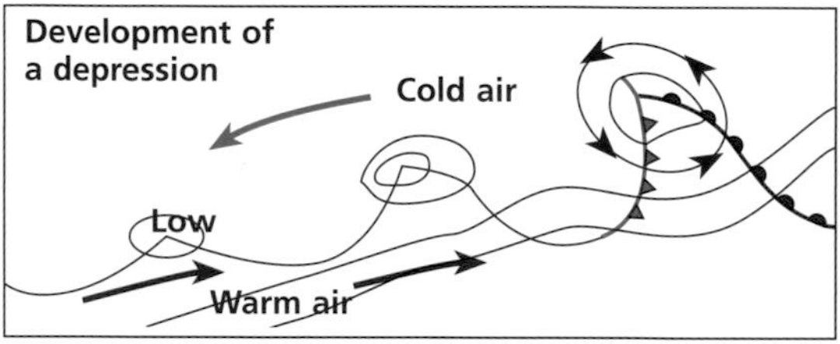

Depressions are bad weather systems with their most turbulent winds occurring at their centres; so it is an advantage to know where the centre of an approaching depression lies in relation to your own position.

Buys Ballot's Law states that if you face the wind in the northern hemisphere, the low pressure centre will be between 90°–135° on your right. 'The crossed winds' rule also provides a rough guide to weather trends: if you face the wind and look up at the clouds to compare the direction of the higher altitude wind. If the cloud comes from the right, the weather is likely to deteriorate. If the movement is from the left, the weather will most likely improve, but if the movement is either directly toward or away from you, then existing conditions will probably remain unchanged.

Weather maps

A weather map shows the distribution of atmospheric pressure throughout an area by means of lines (isobars) drawn through places having the same pressure. The isobaric structure in any area gives an indication of the weather pattern prevailing there, ie isobars are drawn at intervals of 2, 4, or 8mb either side of 1000mb thus forming a pressure contour map similar to a geographical contour map.

The pressure gradient is the rate of change in pressure across the isobars and is analogous to the gradient of a hill. Closely-spaced land contours indicate steep gradients; similarly, closely-spaced isobars portray steep pressure gradients which, in turn, produce stronger winds (*Fig 1*).

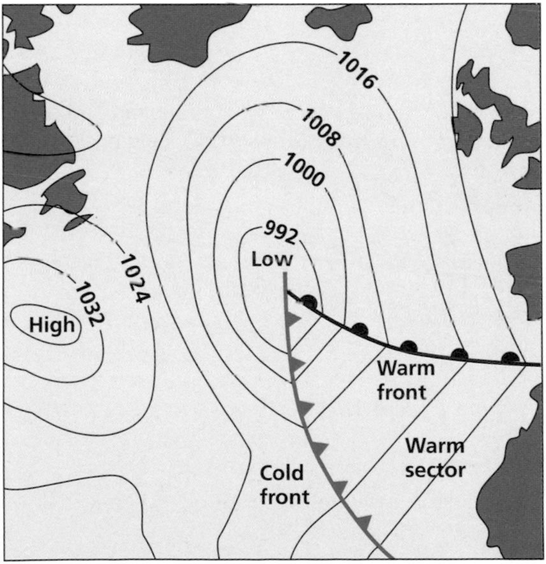

Fig 1

Weather maps

Each isobar forms a closed circuit around a centre of either high or low pressure and in the northern hemisphere, winds above 2000ft blow parallel to the isobars – clockwise around areas of high pressure and anti-clockwise around low pressure areas. Surface winds however are always 'backed' from the direction of the isobars and diverge away from a centre of high pressure but converge toward a centre of low pressure (*Fig 2*).

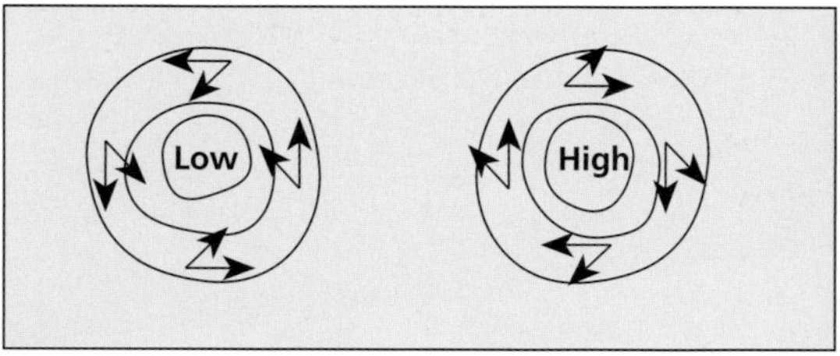

Fig 2

Fig 3 depicts a simple depression in the northern hemisphere with winds blowing anti-clockwise in the general direction of the isobars but backed slightly inwards. From the centre, line A–B represents the warm front – the leading edge of the air in the warm sector which is riding up over the relatively cold air to the right of it. Line A–C is the cold front. This is the leading edge of a wedge of cold air which is pushing into the warm sector ahead of it. In this instance the depression and its fronts are moving steadily from left to right in the general direction of the isobars in the warm sector and if you were at 'X', you might expect to experience the following pattern of events as the depression passes over you.

High cloud from the west increases and lowers as the warm front approaches, pressure falls and the wind strengthens and backs; visibility deteriorates and light rain becomes continuous and heavy. As the warm front passes, pressure steadies, the wind veers, and rain stops or turns to drizzle. In the warm sector (*Fig 4*), visibility is poor with drizzle or showers. Wind and pressure is steady. At the cold front, pressure falls then rises sharply. Wind veers and becomes squally with heavy rain. As the front moves away, rain stops, visibility improves and pressure rises.

Fig 3

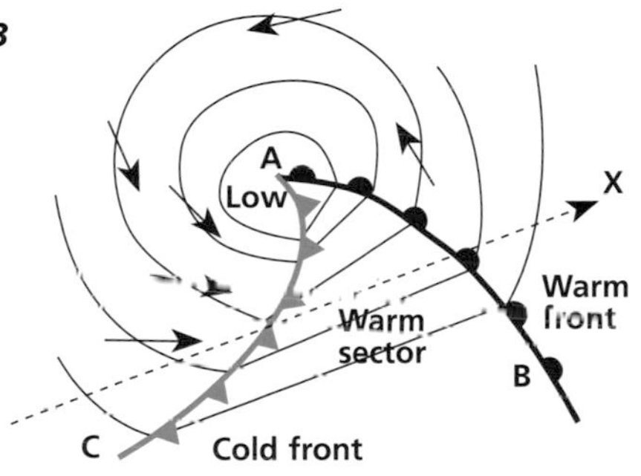

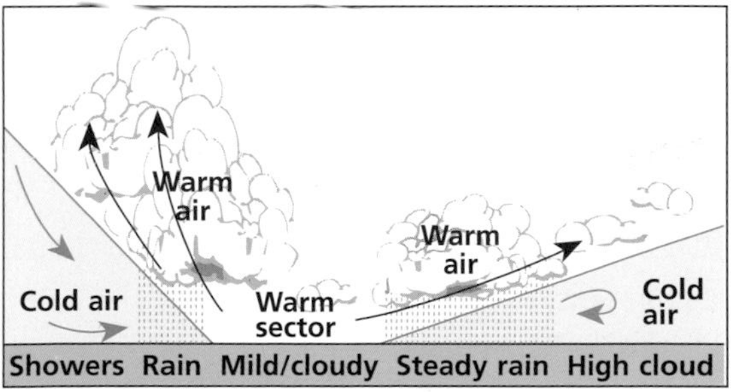

Fig 4 Section through a warm sector depression.

Local winds

Local effects

Wind is moving air created by temperature differences. Local winds in various forms are a modification to the general weather pattern but stem from the same basic cause.

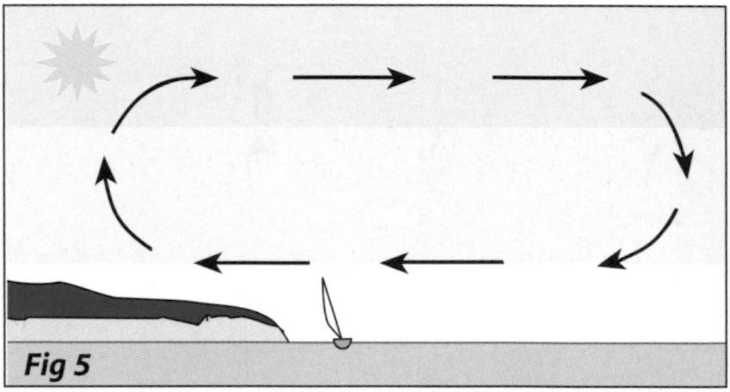

Fig 5

Sea breezes These develop in coastal areas when convection over the land on a warm sunny day causes strong upward currents of air (*Fig 5*). The rising air is replaced by an inflow of air from over the sea which creates an onshore wind.

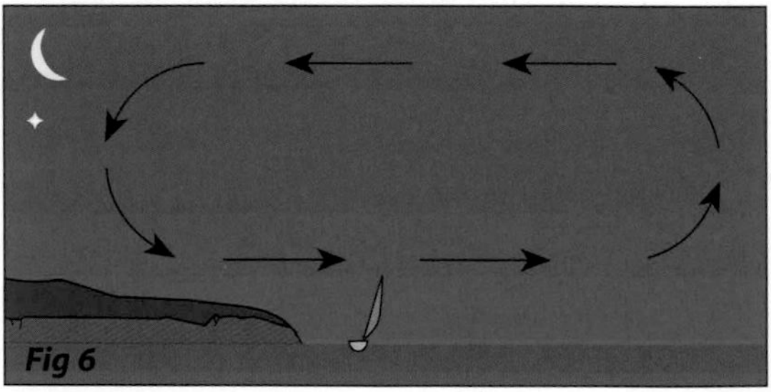

Fig 6

Land breeze At night the process is reversed (*Fig 6*). The Earth cools quickly after sunset while the sea retains its temperature and so air is drawn off the land to replace the warm air rising from over the sea.

Katabatic winds

In areas where the coastline is more dramatic and cloudless skies at night result in radiation cooling of the land, a strong, down-slope wind can develop as air in contact with the ground becomes chilled and flows rapidly down the hillside (*Fig 7*).

Fig 7

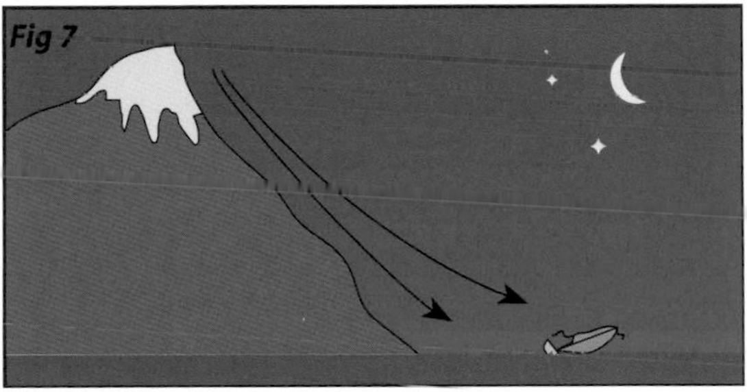

Fog This can form at any time of year but does so most frequently in late spring to mid-summer. It occurs when warm moist air is cooled sufficiently to become saturated and condense into water vapour.

Advection (sea fog) This occurs when warm moist air flows over a relatively cold sea surface and the temperature of the air in contact with this surface is lowered. If the sea temperature is below the dew point temperature of the air and cooling continues until the air is saturated, condensation will take place and form mist or fog.

Radiation (land fog) A clear night sky results in rapid cooling of the land. Should the surface temperature fall below the dew point temperature of the air, saturation will occur and condensation will take place with the formation of fog, which may drift out to sea.

Beaufort scale

Beaufort wind force scale

Force	*Knots*	*Wind*	*Probable sea state*
1	1–3	Light airs	Ripples
2	4–6	Light breeze	Small wavelets
3	7–10	Gentle breeze	Crests begin to break
4	11–16	Mod breeze	Waves becoming larger, frequent white crests
5	17–21	Fresh breeze	Mod waves, many white crests, some spray
6	22–27	Strong breeze	Large waves, extensive white crests
7	28–33	Near gale	Sea heaps up, waves breaking white foam blown in streaks
8	34–40	Gale	Mod high waves, crests break into spindrift, white foam
9	41–47	Strong gale	High waves, crests topple spray affects visibility
10	48–55	Storm	Very high breaking waves, dense foam streaks

▶▶ Caution

Originally devised for larger sailing craft, this scale is only a rough guide to what may be expected in open water. Wind speeds are averages and gusts up to the next force should be anticipated. Sea conditions are generally more severe nearer to land and wave height can increase dramatically within minutes.

You should never venture outside sheltered waters unless you have obtained a current weather forecast and can interpret it correctly.

BBC radio shipping forecasts

Shipping forecasts are broadcast by BBC Radio 4 on LW (1515m, 198 kHz) and Radio 4 FM at 0048, 0520, 1201* and 1754 (local time).

Reports from coastal stations are now only given with 0048 and 0520 forecasts.

*Radio 4 FM (weekends only)

Note Broadcast times are subject to change.

Gale warnings

These are given at programme junctions following their issue and after each hourly news bulletin. Warnings remain in force until cancelled or if persisting for more than 24 hours the warnings are re-issued.

- A gale warning indicates that winds of at least force 8–34kn (gusting to 43kn) are expected in the area.
- A *severe gale* implies winds of force 9 with wind gusting up to 50kn. A *storm* implies winds of force 10 gusting to 60kn.
- Wind direction is given as the direction ***from*** which it is blowing and is defined by compass point rather than 360° notation.

Wind shifts

In the Northern hemisphere a wind is said to ***back*** when it shifts to blow from a more anti-clockwise direction and to ***veer*** if it shifts to blow from a direction more clockwise.

A backing wind usually indicates the approach of bad weather, while a veering wind signals the approach of better weather.

Shipping forecasts

Meaning of shipping forecast terms

Timing of gale warnings

◆ *Imminent*	Within 6 hours of time of issue
◆ *Soon*	6 to 12 hours
◆ *Later*	12 to 24 hours

Visibility

◆ *Good*	More than 5 miles
◆ *Moderate*	2 to 5 miles
◆ *Poor*	1100 yards to 2 miles
◆ *Fog*	Less than 1100 yards

Pressure tendency

◆ *Steady*	Change less than 0·1mb in 3hrs
◆ *Rising or falling slowly*	Change 0·1 to 1·5mb in last 3hrs
◆ *Rising or falling*	Change 1·6 to 3·5mb in last 3hrs
◆ *Rising or falling quickly*	Change 3·6 to 6·0mb in last 3hrs
◆ *Rising or falling very rapidly*	Change of more than 6·0mb in last 3hrs
◆ *Now rising or falling*	Change within the last 3hrs

Speed of movement

◆ *Slowly*	up to 15kn
◆ *Steadily*	15 to 25kn
◆ *Rather quickly*	25 to 35kn
◆ *Rapidly*	35 to 45kn
◆ *Very rapidly*	over 45kn

Other weather forecast sources

- **The Met Office** This provides weather information for sailors via phone, fax, internet and mobile phone. There is also the facility to obtain direct access to a Met Office forecaster if the need arises.

  For a free Met Office booklet detailing these services, telephone 0845 300 0300 or go to www.metoffice.gov.uk/leisuremarine

- **Coastguard** Inshore waters forecasts are announced on VHF CH16; normally broadcast on VHF CH23, 84 or 86).

- **NAVTEX** An electronic news and weather information system. (A dedicated onboard receiver is needed.)

- **Internet** Provides forecasts for UK inshore waters.

  Met Office – www.meto.gov.uk
  Online weather – www.onlineweather.com

- **Television** TV weather maps provide a useful overview of general weather trends.

- **CEEFAX** and **TELETEXT** For the latest weather updates.

- **Harbour office** This will give the latest local weather conditions.

✷ Top tip
Always check the weather forecast before you go and be prepared to change your plans. And remember, if in doubt – don't go!

Anchors

Choice of anchor

CQR, Danforth and Bruce anchors have largely replaced the 'traditional' Fisherman pattern as main anchor because they offer more holding power for less weight. It is the composition of the sea bed, however, that finally determines whether or not any particular type of anchor will hold well. Although a smaller, lighter anchor may hold securely in an 'ideal bottom', it will almost certainly drag if the ground is very soft, or if it is too hard for the anchor to penetrate. It is then the weight of the anchor that matters, rather than its resistance to drag.

In general, anchors hold best in hard mud, clay or sand and less well in soft mud, gravel and shingle. Holding in weed or on rock is always unreliable.

Fisherman This anchor must be heavy to be effective but it is the only one which will hold at all well on a rocky sea bed. Can be stowed flat.

CQR High holding-to-weight ratio. Designed to burrow. Good in sand and mud, not so good on hard sand or in weed. Awkward to stow.

Danforth Good holding-to-weight ratio. Holds well in soft sand and mud. Not good on hard sand or in weed. Can often be hard to break out of sea bed. Stows flat.

Bruce Very high holding-to-weight ratio. Good in sand or mud. Awkward to stow.

✱ Top tip

Cruising boats should carry a large *main anchor*, preferably rigged with chain, and a smaller *kedge anchor* with a chain leader and a long *nylon warp*. Having main and kedge anchors of different types gives a choice to suit varying sea bed composition.

Common types of anchor

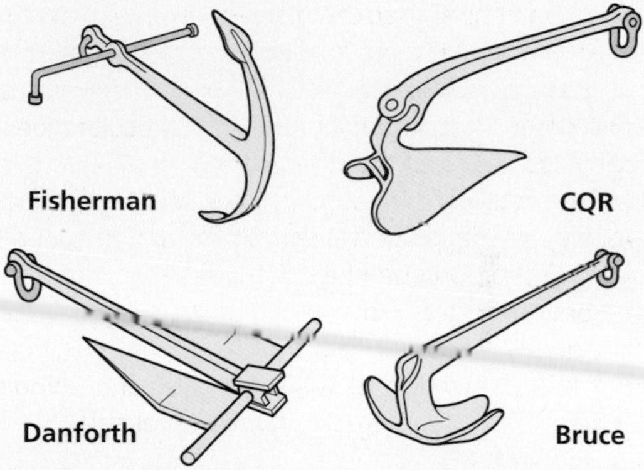

Fig 1 ***(Not to scale)***

Suggested anchor weights (guide only)			
Boat length *mtrs*	**Bruce** *kg*	**Danforth/ CQR** *kg*	**Chain** *mm*
6–8	5	8	8
9	7.5	14	8
10	10	14	10
11	10	14	10
12	15	19	10
14	20	25	12
16	20	25	12
18	30	34	12

Kedge anchor

Usually of a different type and about 20% lighter than the main anchor, rigged with a 6m chain 'leader' and a long nylon warp of suitable strength.

Anchors

Anchor cables

These can be of either chain or rope, but for any type of anchor to be effective, the pull on its cable must lie ***parallel to the sea bed***. The weight of a chain ensures a horizontal pull and its catenary (curve) provides a damping effect as the yacht surges against its anchor. If a nylon warp is used, at least six metres of chain should be connected between it and the anchor. The stretch in nylon rope acts as a damper, but it is light and a weight may be needed to increase the catenary and improve the horizontal pull (*Fig 2* opposite).

Where to anchor

A suitable place to anchor should be well protected with little or no tidal stream and have good holding ground. Recommended anchorages are printed on charts or are indicated by the chart symbol ⚓.

Depth of water and composition of the sea bed is also shown (*Fig 3*). ***Never anchor off a lee shore***.

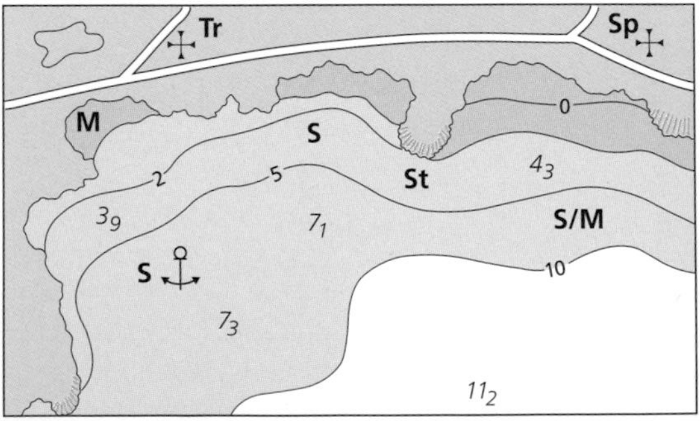

Fig 3

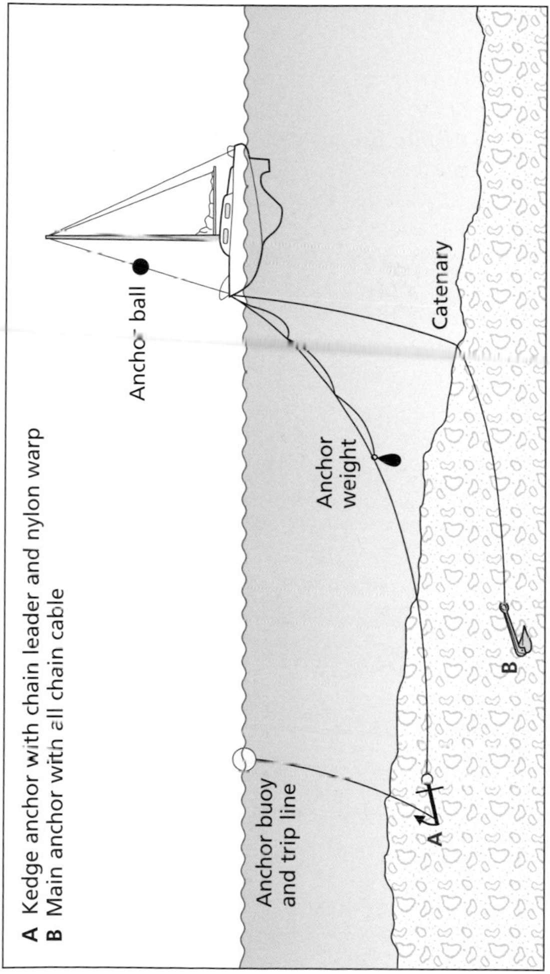
A Kedge anchor with chain leader and nylon warp
B Main anchor with all chain cable
Anchor ball
Anchor weight
Catenary
Anchor buoy and trip line
A
B

Fig 2

Anchoring

Anchoring technique

When you have found a suitable anchorage, motor in and have a good look around. Choose a spot where your boat will have ample room to swing around its anchor without fouling anything or colliding with any boats that are already there. If you have any doubts, remember that the 'first boat in has right of stay' – so it's up to you to find another spot.

Have everything prepared in advance. Hang the anchor over the bow roller, secured but ready to let go. Flake out the required amount of cable on to the deck and secure the inboard end to a cleat or the samson post.

You will need at least six times the maximum depth of water expected if your cable is rope or four times the depth if it is all chain (see page 82).

Make your approach into the strongest element – wind or tide – and motor a short distance beyond the spot where you want your boat to lie; put the engine in neutral and once the boat has stopped, lower the anchor smoothly to the bottom and pay out the cable as the boat drifts back. When all the cable is out, a short burst astern with the engine will usually set the anchor.

After the boat has settled down and appears to be riding to the anchor, and before you switch off the engine, take bearings on one or two fixed objects ashore and check them periodically for any change that would suggest a dragging anchor. Finally, rig an anchor ball or light as required by the Colreg (see page 113).

✷ Top tip

If you are unable to take bearings for any reason, suspend a sounding lead from the bow, leaving some slack in the line. Check the line every few minutes without lifting the weight from the bottom. If the line is still vertical, your anchor is holding, but if the line is sloping out ahead, it is dragging.

Using two anchors

A boat lying to a single anchor will have a large swinging circle and should not be left unattended. In crowded anchorages in calm conditions, the circle can be reduced by using two anchors laid out over the bow with the heaviest anchor towards the strongest tidal stream (*Fig 4*).

Drop the main anchor as before and allow the boat to drift back as you pay out ***twice*** the required length of cable. Lower the second anchor and pull the boat forward again by hauling in the main cable while paying out the second anchor's cable until the boat is positioned midway between the two anchors. Make the second cable fast to the main cable and let them out until the joint is ***well below the keel depth.***

▶▶ Caution

In strong cross winds both anchors may drag.

Fig 4

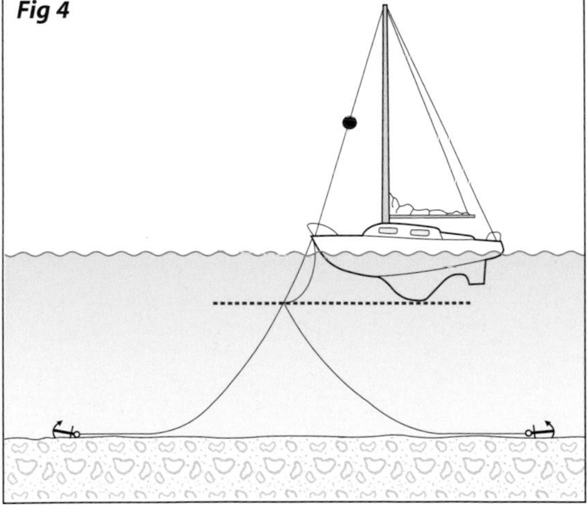

Anchoring

Windy conditions

When strong winds are expected, and the boat will be wind-rode rather than tide-rode, a safer method of lying to two anchors is to drop the main anchor as before, allow the boat to drift back to set the anchor, and then motor off at an angle of about 40° to the line of the first anchor and drop the kedge level with it (*Fig 5*). Allow the boat to drift back again, then adjust and cleat the cables securely.

Fig 5

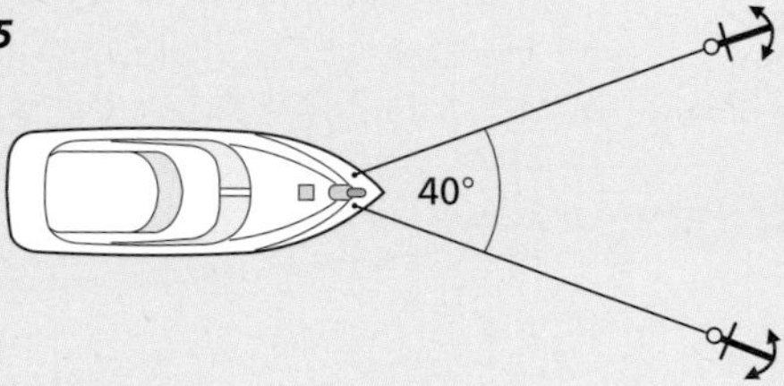

✷ Top tip

To secure a cable (rope or chain) to a samson post, take three turns round the post, pass a bight of cable under the part attached to the anchor and slip it over the turns on the post. For extra security, take the end round the post again and repeat the process with a second bight of cable. A rope or chain secured in this way will not jam and can be released under load.

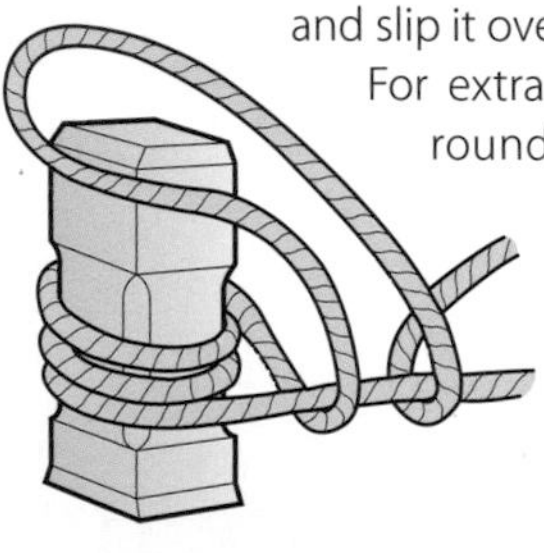

Fouled anchor

Never anchor near underwater cables or pipelines and avoid places on the chart marked 'Foul Ground' where there will be obstructions upon which an anchor might become fast.

An anchor buoy with a trip line attached to the crown of the anchor will provide a means of freeing it; but it is not unknown for an unwary skipper to try to moor up to someone else's anchor buoy, and there is also a danger that the line may foul your rudder at low water and trip the anchor later as the tide rises. For these reasons, you may prefer to lash the tripping line to your anchor cable and bring the buoy back on board.

Fig 6

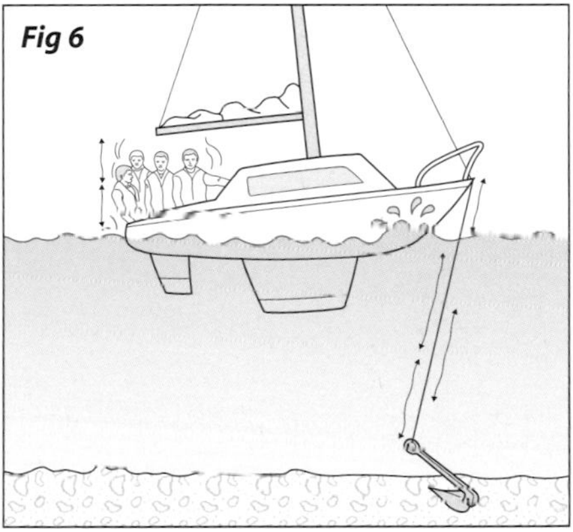

If you have no tripping line set and the anchor becomes fast, haul the cable in until it is vertical and taut, take a turn around a cleat, move all the crew right aft and see if the motion of the boat will break it out (*Fig 6*). If not, try motoring in the opposite direction from which the anchor was originally set or veer a little more cable, then keeping it taut, motor in a circle around your anchor to see if that will free it.

Mooring alongside

When nearing your intended berth, note the direction and strength of wind and tide and make your approach into the strongest element. Check for obstructions or warning notices, rig adequate fenders and if the quay has projecting buttresses, rig a fender board to bridge the gaps (*Fig 7*).

Mooring lines

The lines needed to hold a boat against a quay or pontoon, or alongside another boat are generally positioned as shown (*Fig 8*). Bow and stern lines hold the boat in position while springs prevent her from surging back and forth. Breast ropes hold the boat close in but are rarely necessary on small craft and they must ***never*** be left unattended on a boat berthed against a tidal quay.

Unless your boat is moored to a floating pontoon, ensure that all your other lines are long enough to allow for the range of the tide. Bow and stern lines should be at least three times as long as the predicted range and springs one and a half times the range.

✱ Top tip

If you expect to be away from the boat while the tide is ebbing and you are uncertain about the range of tide at your mooring, or the amount of slack you need to leave in the lines, just make a bight in one of the lines and double it, then put on a 'seizing' of some easily breaking stuff such as ordinary string. If the lines are then subject to any undue strain, the string will break and allow another metre or so of slack (*Fig 9*).

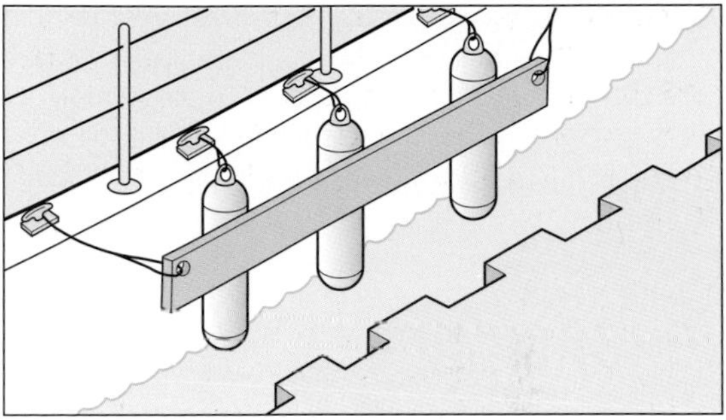

Fig 7

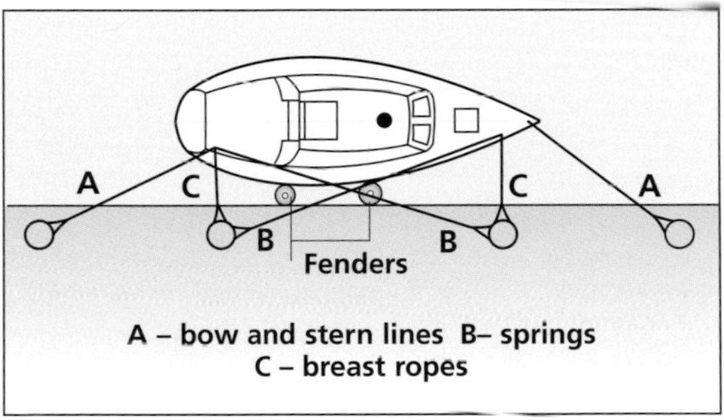

Fig 8

Fig 9

Mooring alongside

Mooring rings and bollards

A line is best attached to a mooring ring with a round turn and two half hitches (*Fig 10*). This knot is very secure and can be released while under tension.

A bowline is best for making fast to a bollard, but always pass the loop up through any others that are there before dropping it over the bollard (*Fig 11*). The lines can then be released in any order just by lifting the appropriate loop off the bollard and dropping it back through the others.

Fig 10

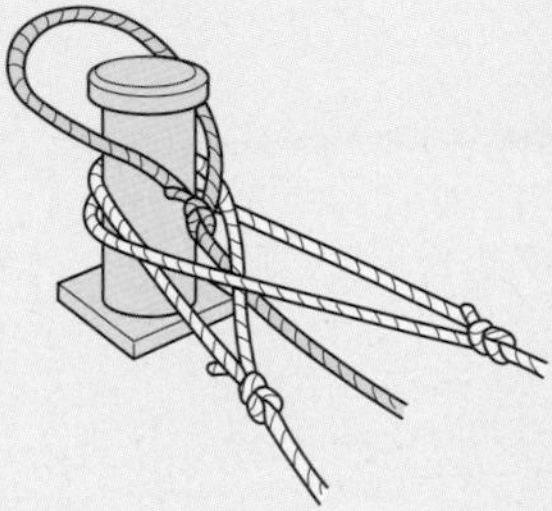

Fig 11

- Protect your lines from 'chafe' where they are likely to rub on the rough stone edges of a tidal quay.
- Route all mooring lines through fairleads on the boat and secure them to deck cleats so that the load is taken along their length, ***not*** across them.
- Check to see if any mooring lines are likely to snag and dislodge the fenders.

Slip ropes

When preparing to leave a berth, you can rig mooring lines as *slip ropes* by doubling them back through a ring or round a cleat or bollard on shore so you can let them go from on board, but slip ropes are liable to jam if they are not rigged or handled correctly.

- When slipping from a ringbolt, pass the line down through a ring which hangs from a quayside but up through a ring which lies on top of a quay.
- Always let go the shortest end of the rope and haul in steadily.
- Do not jerk the rope, especially when the end is nearing the ring or bollard.

Mooring alongside another boat

It doesn't usually matter which way you face in relation to the other boat, ask permission to come alongside and head into the strongest element: wind or tide. Provide adequate fenders; rig springs and breast ropes to the other boat and haul them tight. If the boats are facing the same way, adjust the springs to put the masts out of line in case the boats roll, and ***take your own bow and stern lines ashore*** (*Fig 12*). Don't rely on the other boat's lines to hold you.

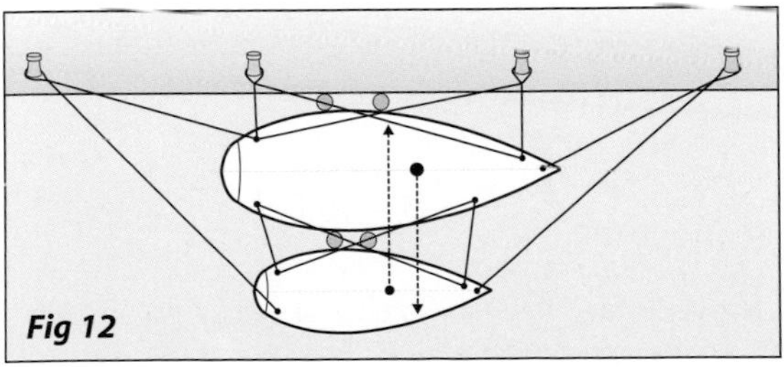

Fig 12

Mooring alongside

Leaving a raft of boats

To leave from a berth in the middle of a raft of boats, you must rearrange the mooring lines of the adjacent boats so that you can leave in the direction of the strongest element (wind or tide) so that its force will cause the other boats to swing together as you leave. If you attempt to leave ***against a strong wind or tide***, the raft will be torn apart and boats may be damaged (*Fig 13*).

Fig 13

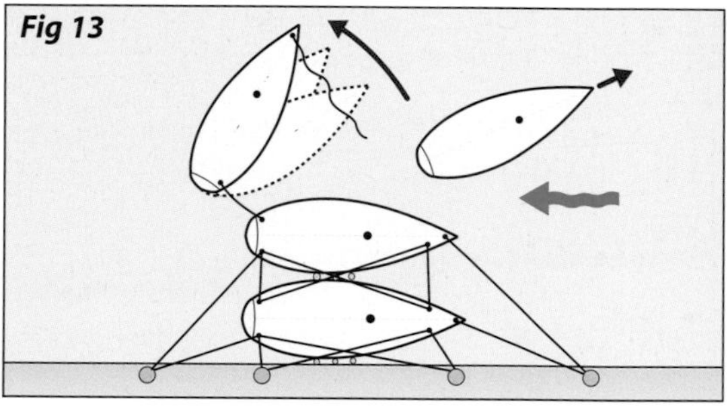

To leave a raft (bows first)

1. Have your engine running in neutral. Take in your bow and stern lines, remove your springs from the inside boat and make up the breast ropes as slip lines.
2. Unfasten the bow line of the boat lying outside you at the mooring and lead it right round your own boat, outside the guardrail and shrouds and back to the shore, extending the line if necessary (*Fig 15*).
3. Cast off the springs and breast ropes of the outside boat, make a final check for any forgotten ropes, snagged fenders, or rope dangling in the water, then slip your breast ropes from the inside boat and gently ease your boat out with the current (*Fig 16*). If there is no one aboard the other boats to help you, you will have to leave one of your crew behind to secure their lines, and pick him up later.

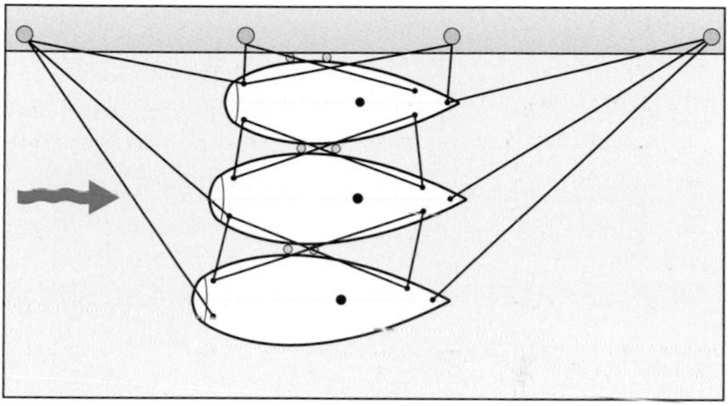

Fig 14

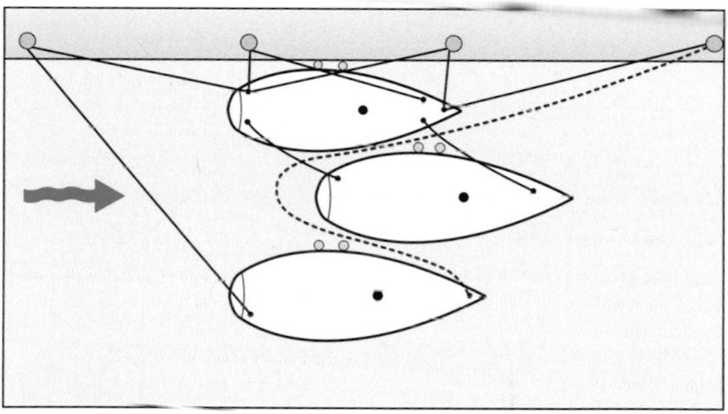

Fig 15

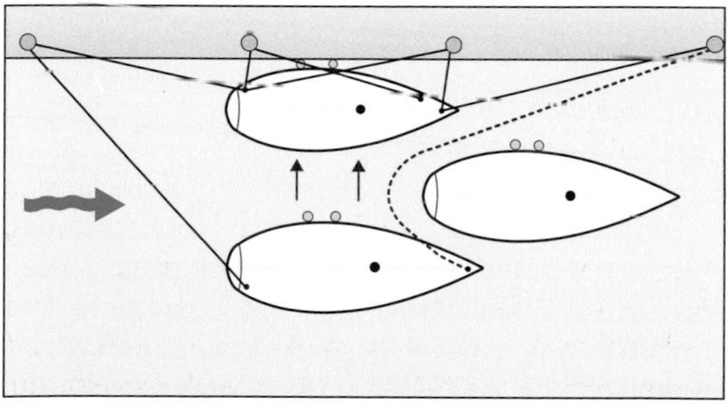

Fig 16

Leaving a berth

Leaving an alongside berth when there is little or no wind or tidal stream

If your boat is docked closely between other boats and you are short-handed, or your boat is too heavy to push off with the boat-hook, try 'springing it off' using your engine and a suitable mooring line.

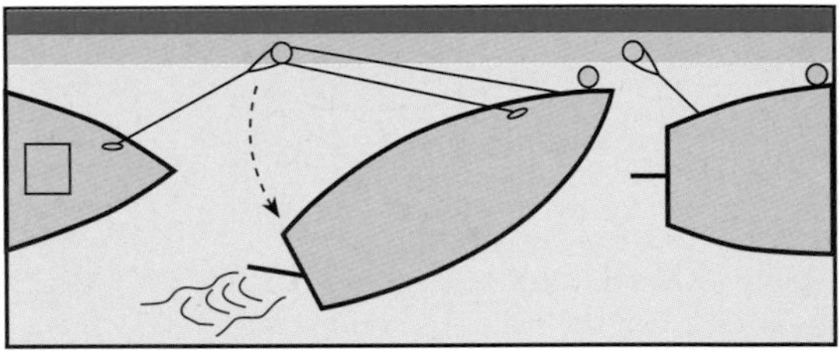

***Fig 17** Rig your bow spring as a 'slip' and position a fender well forward between the bow and the quay. Gently engage forward drive with rudder turned towards the quay and the stern will begin to swing out. Once you are clear of the boat behind, slip and retrieve the spring and reverse away.*

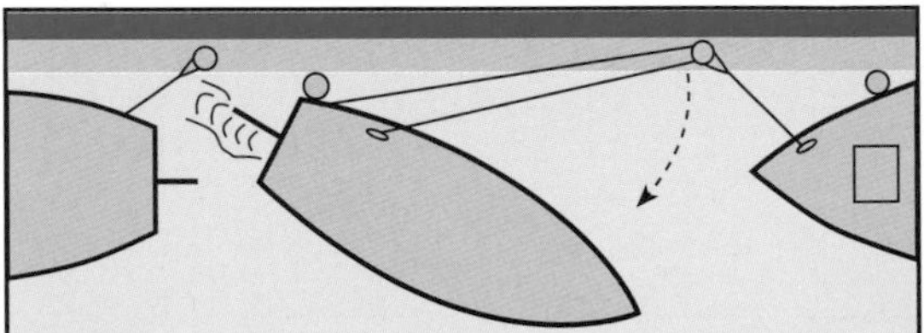

***Fig 18** Rig a stern spring as a 'slip' and position a fender well aft between the boat and the quay. Centralise the rudder and gently engage astern drive. The bow will begin to swing out and when it is clear of the boat ahead, slip and retrieve the spring and motor ahead and away.*

Using the tidal stream to leave an alongside berth

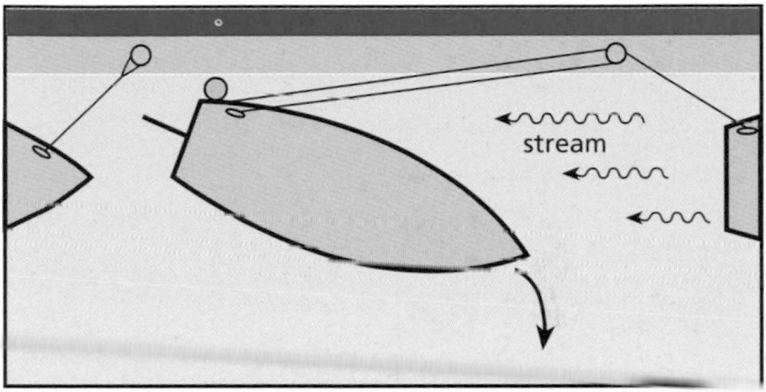

***Fig 19** With the tidal stream on the bow, position a fender aft and rig the stern spring as a 'slip'. Remove the bow lines and the effect of the tidal stream will cause the bow to swing out. When clear of any boat ahead, engage forward drive, slip and retrieve the stern spring and motor ahead and away.*

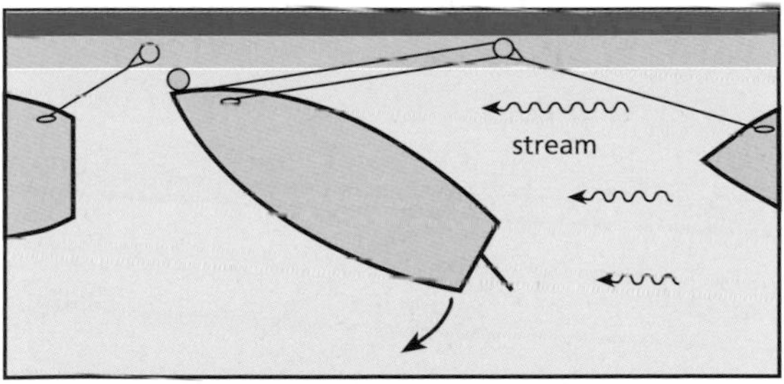

***Fig 20** With the tidal stream from astern, position a fender well forward and rig the bow spring as a 'slip'. Remove the stern lines and the effect of the tidal stream will cause the stern to swing out. When clear of any boat behind you, engage astern propulsion, slip and retrieve the bow spring and reverse away.*

How sails work

It is possible to sail a boat 'upwind' chiefly because its sails are designed to assume an aerofoil shape when the wind strikes them. Air flowing over the curved leeward side of the sail accelerates, decreasing the pressure on that surface and creating a partial vacuum or suction effect called 'lift' which tends to drive the boat forward (*Fig 1*).

Fig 1

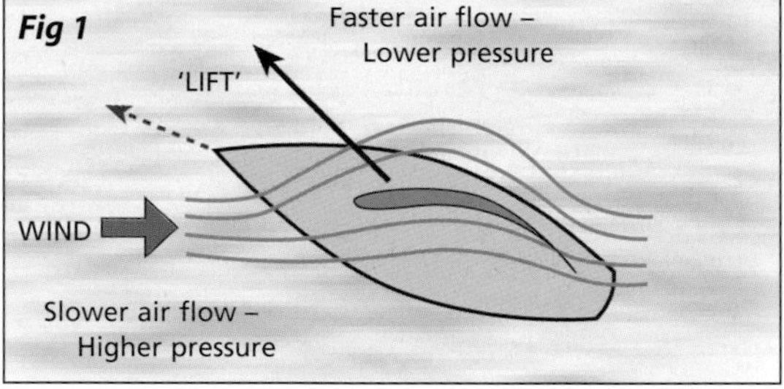

Wind pressure on the other side of the sail gives it its curved shape and also creates a force that tries to push the boat downwind. But this sideways movement (leeway) is resisted by the keel and rudder and so the forward 'lift' of the sail predominates and, combined with a similar forward 'lift' generated by the keel which functions as a 'hydrofoil', the boat is driven in that direction (*Fig 2*).

Fig 2

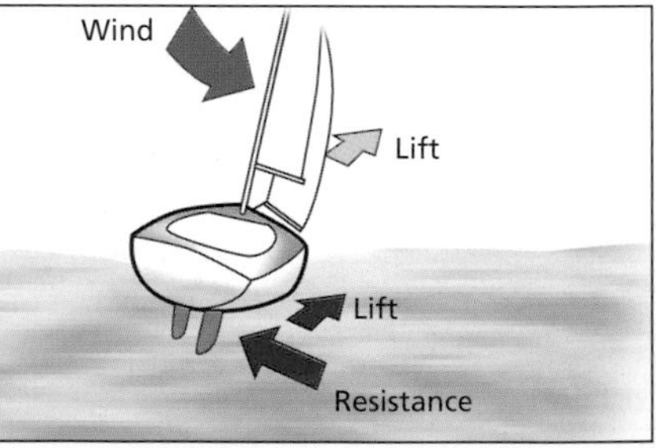

The 'slot' effect

The faster that the air can be made to flow over the curved surface of a sail, the greater will be the 'lift' created. This condition is met, when beating or reaching, by an overlap between the headsail and the luff of the main which creates a 'slot effect' to squeeze and speed up the airflow through the gap between the sails (*Fig 3*).

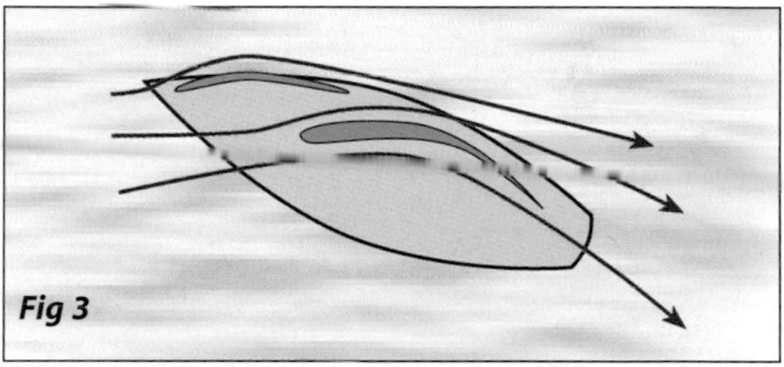

Fig 3

In general, the narrower the slot, the faster the airflow (*Fig 4*), but this must not be overdone or the air-stream from the leech of the headsail will 'backwind' the luff of the mainsail (*Fig 5*) and destroy its lift completely.

The mainsail needs to be sheeted in slightly harder than the headsail, but try to keep the slot between the two sails even so that their leeches follow a similar curve.

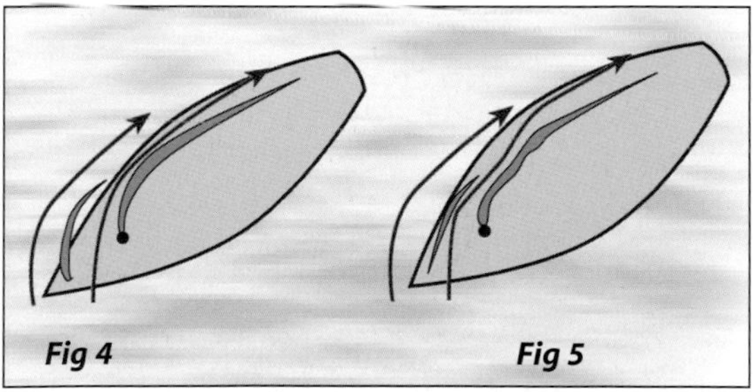

Fig 4 **Fig 5**

Apparent wind

All moving vehicles experience a 'speed wind' blowing in the opposite direction to that in which the vehicle is moving (*Fig 6*).

Fig 6

Even on a windless day, a cyclist will feel a wind on his face caused solely by his movement through the still air and the faster he pedals, the stronger that wind will become (*Fig 7*).

Fig 7

On a windy day, the wind that is felt by the crew of a moving yacht is a combination of the true wind and the speed wind and is known to sailors as the 'apparent wind'. This is the wind to which the sails are trimmed and its direction is invariably forward of the true wind's direction.

In sailing, especially sailboat racing, apparent wind is a vitally important factor, since it determines the points of sail on which the sails can most efficiently generate forward motion.

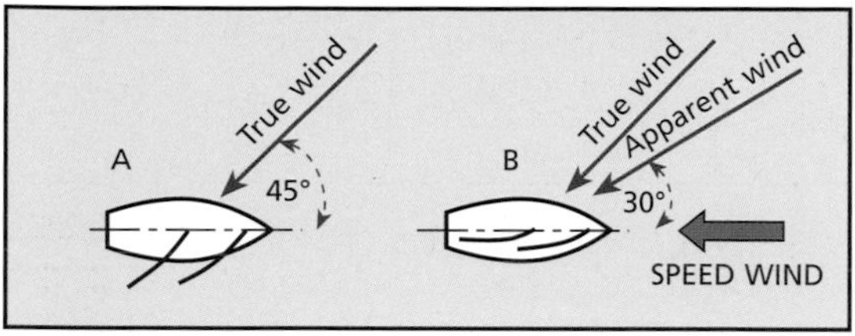

Fig 8

Most boats are unable to sail closer than about 45° to the true wind **A** but once the boat begins to move and pick up speed, the apparent wind strengthens and moves forward and the sails are trimmed accordingly as in **B** (*Fig 8*).

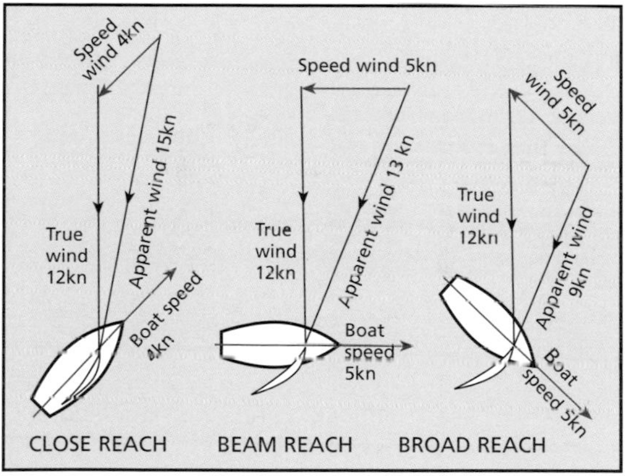

Fig 9

Given a true wind of constant velocity, the velocity and direction of the apparent wind varies with the speed of the vessel and its point of sailing, as shown by the vector diagrams (*Fig 9*).

Points of sailing

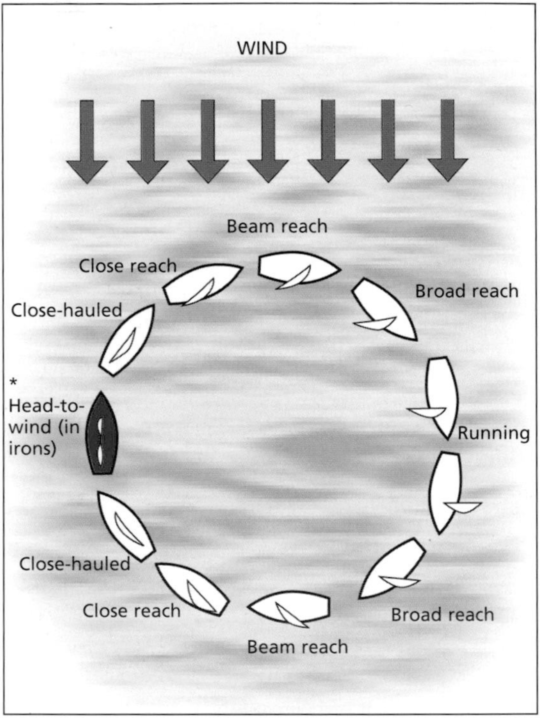

A boat cannot sail directly into the wind; its sails would 'flog' uselessly. They need to be set at an angle to the wind to enable them to assume an aerodynamic shape and develop drive. In order to reach an objective dead to windward, the boat must be sailed on a zig-zag course towards it, close-hauled on alternate tacks with the wind first on one side of the boat and then the other. The sails are sheeted in as tightly as possible, and the boat is sailed as close to the wind as it will go without losing drive in the sails.

Beating, reaching and running

These are terms used to describe a boat's course relative to the wind direction.

Beating No sailing boat is able to sail directly into the wind and few can sail closer to the true wind than about 45°. This term describes a boat that is sailing as close to the wind as possible with its sails sheeted in tightly (close-hauled).

Reaching is any point of sailing between that of beating or running. The boat is said to be on a **close reach** when it is no longer close-hauled or 'hard on the wind'. It is on a **beam reach** when the sails are eased further out and the wind is at roughly right-angles to its course, and it is on a **broad reach** when the wind blows over the quarter ('aft' of the beam).

Running is when the boat is sailing directly down wind with its sails eased out to their furthest extent. When running, the headsail is in the lee of the main and does no work so it is often 'poled out' on the opposite side to catch the wind – generally known as 'goose winging'. Great care must be taken when running dead before the wind since there is always the danger of an involuntary gybe. If the wind should catch the sail from the other side it may cause the boom to scythe across the deck and strike anyone in its path.

A boat's speed increases as it moves from close-hauled to reaching and a broad reach can be the fastest point of sailing if extra sail is set. Beyond this point, the apparent wind diminishes, the boat slows and a dead run is the slowest point of all.

Knots

The dividing line between knots, bends and hitches is not precise. In general, most knots are formed in the end of a rope as a 'stopper' or 'binder', a bend is used to join the ends of two ropes and a hitch is used to secure a rope to some other object.

Figure of eight knot A single strand stopper put on the end of a sheet or halyard to prevent the end unreeving (*Fig 1*).

Fig 1

Reef knot A binder knot used for tying in 'reef points' or when furling sails. To undo quickly, jerk one end away from its own standing part (*Fig 2*) and the knot will capsize into a cow hitch which will easily slide off the rope's end.

Fig 2

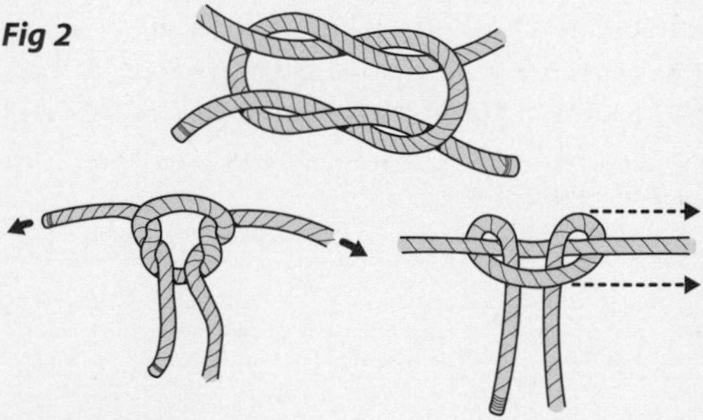

Caution

Do not use a reef knot as a 'bend' for tying two ropes together. If the ropes are of different sizes or materials, or if one is stiffer than the other, the knot is very liable to fail.

Bowline knot Undoubtedly this is the sailor's most useful knot. Used to form a standing loop in the end of a line, it will not jam, slip or capsize. It is easy to undo when not under load (*Fig 3*).

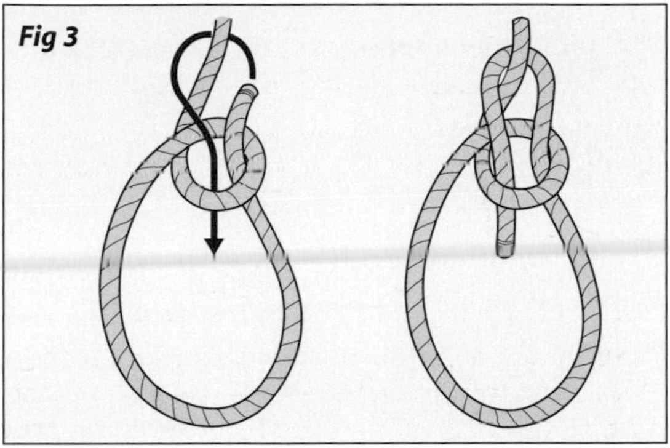

Fig 3

Half hitch (*Fig 4*): Although it will not hold on its own without a seizing, it is the basis for several other knots, one of which is the **round turn and two half hitches** (*Fig 5*), the most commonly used hitch for securing a rope to a post or bollard. It is easily untied. ***Seize the end if it is used aloft***.

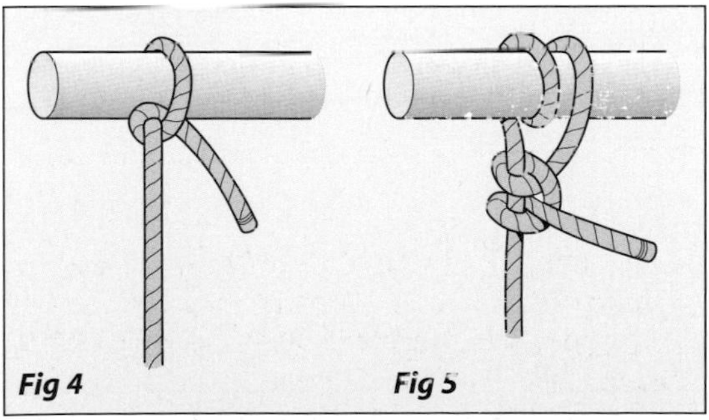

Fig 4 **Fig 5**

Hitches

Clove hitch Used to secure a line to a spar or post, this hitch is only secure if a load is applied to both sides of the knot (*Fig 6*). It tends to unwind with a steady pull to one side only unless the free end of the line is seized, or finished off with a couple of half hitches.

Fig 6

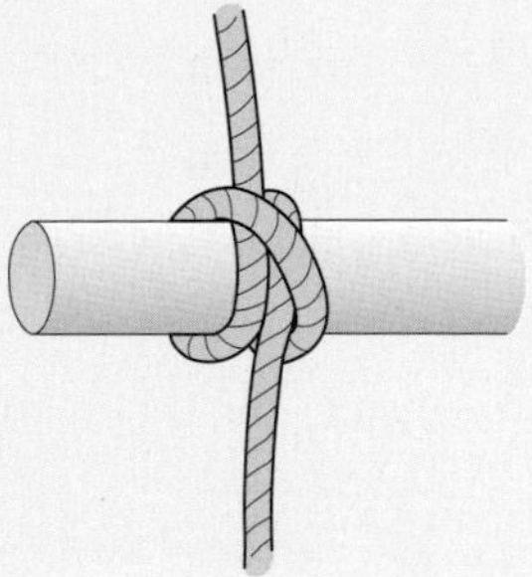

Rolling hitch Used to attach a line to a spar, or a larger rope, when the direction of 'pull' is along the rope or spar (*Fig 7*). It is basically a clove hitch with an extra turn inserted on that side of the 'clove' to which the hitch must not slide.

Fig 7

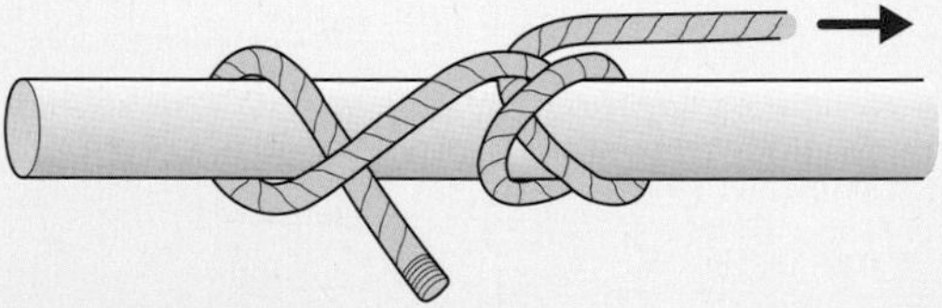

Fisherman's (or anchor) bend A variation of the round turn and two half hitches and is used to secure a rope to a ring or an anchor (*Fig 8*). It is easy to undo, even when it has been strained, and will not jam if the loose end is stopped back to the standing part of the rope.

Fig 8

Sheet bend (*Fig 9*) Used to attach the end of one rope to the end of another. The **double sheet bend** (*Fig 10*) is more secure when one rope is much thinner than the other. To join rope of different materials, the ends should be seized to prevent the bend from 'spilling'.

Fig 9

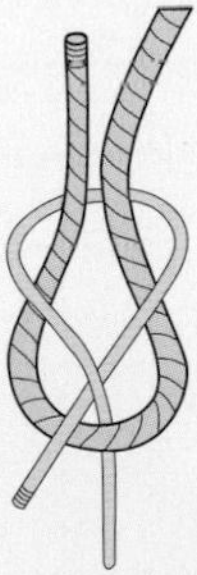

Fig 10

Bends

Sheepshank (*Fig 11*) Used to temporarily shorten a rope where both ends of the rope are made fast. It can be used to take the strain off a damaged rope by ensuring that the damaged part lies on the section of rope between the two loops – **X**. *The sheepshank will fall apart if the load comes off the rope unless each bight is secured to the standing part with a seizing.*

Fig 11

The Klemheist knot (*Fig 12*) More familiar to climbers perhaps, it has many uses on board as a 'rolling stopper'. The strop is easily fashioned from a short length of suitable line **A** and has the advantage that when it is attached to another rope as shown in **B** the knot will slide in either direction but when a strain is put on the eye of the knot as in **C** it will not slip.

Fig 12

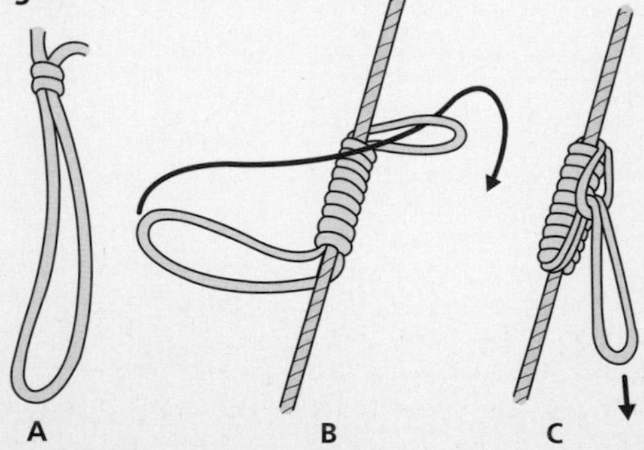

Cleating sheets and halyards

To cleat a halyard, apply a full turn (**1**) followed by one half turn (**2**) and a twisted 'locking' turn (**3**) for extra security. It *is unwise to use a locking turn when cleating a sheet; you may need to free it in a hurry.* Just apply a full turn, one half turn, and finish off with another full turn.

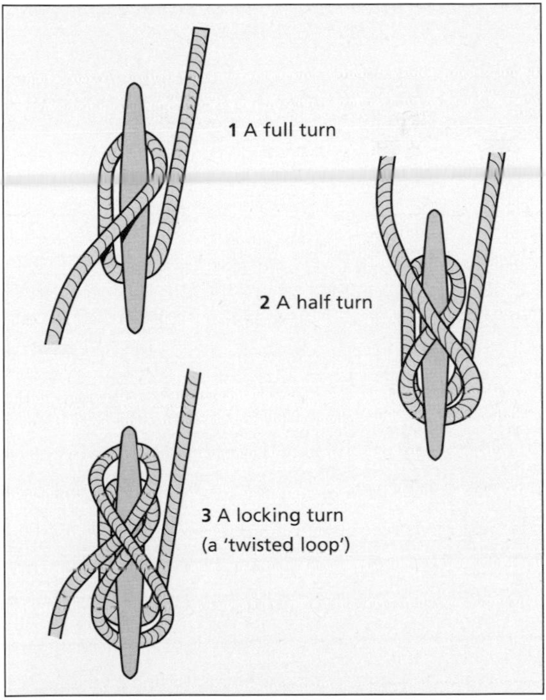

▶▶ Note

If a rope becomes jammed on a cleat it is usually because the full turn is missing – there are too many half turns – or the locking turn has been put on 'back to front'.

Rope – characteristics and uses

Nylon (Enkalon, Polyamide) Rope used for anchoring, mooring and towing lines. It is very strong with good resistance to wear and ultraviolet degradation. Good elastic and shock-absorbing qualities, but not very acid resistant and tends to go stiff when wet, especially in three-strand larger diameter sizes. The plaited version is more flexible. *Nylon does not float.*

Polyester (Terylene, Dacron) This is used for mooring lines. It is almost as strong as nylon, but not as elastic. Also supplied 'pre-stretched' or braided for halyards, sheets, reefing and control lines to give very low-stretch qualities where needed most. It has excellent chemical and ultraviolet resistance, good flexibility and wear resistance but *it does not float*.

Polypropylene (Merkalon, Betelow, Novolen) A rope used for mooring lines and other general purposes. It comes in split film, monofilament, multifilament and staple types. It is not as strong as polyester, and has a stretch factor between nylon and polyester depending on type. It has excellent chemical resistance but poor resistance to ultraviolet light. Polypropylene has fairly good wear resistance. The monofilament type is prone to 'splintering' with age. *All types float.*

Kevlar This is used for halyards, sheets, guys and control lines. It has very high tensile strength and extremely low-stretch qualities, but low resistance to ultraviolet light therefore it is usually sheathed in polyester. It is fire proof but *does not float*.

General stowage and care of rope Use the 'figure of eight' for stowing braided ropes, but 'coil' three-strand rope. Washing rope in fresh water removes dirt, grit, and salt. *Beware of mechanical damage*. Avoid chafe by routeing ropes through fairleads and protect ropes that may rub on rough edges of quays or piers. *Remember that knots can reduce the strength of a rope by as much as 50 per cent.*

Licences

British inland waterways are a relic of the industrial revolution, former trade routes now largely given over to pleasure craft. British Waterways manages more than 2000 miles of canals and rivers (see their website at www.waterscape.com). The Environment Agency together with other Canal Trusts and Authorities administer the remainder. All boats using the waterways must be licensed and have a Boat Safety Scheme certificate. The charge for a British Waterways licence is based on the length of the boat and includes a 'reciprocal use' agreement with some, but not all of the other waterway authorities.

Seagoing craft of suitable dimensions can access parts of the waterways from several points around the coast, but any restrictions imposed by depths of water, clearance under bridges or lock size should be established beforehand. Some equipment not normally carried by seagoing craft should be obtained:

Equipment

- Metal spikes for mooring to the bank.
- A gang plank, for use when the boat cannot be moored close in and a fairly long, stout pole for 'pushing off'.
- Extra fenders will be needed in locks.
- A windlass for lock gate paddle gear.
- A 'headlight' for dark tunnels.
- Anchoring is not permitted on most canals but on fast flowing rivers, keep an anchor ready anyway, for use as a 'handbrake' in case of engine failure etc and a 'mud weight' could be useful where there is little or no current.
- You will also need maps of the canals and rivers concerned to pinpoint the location of locks, weirs, bridges, moorings, water, sanitation and refuse points.

Buoyage and traffic lights

Canals do not have, or need, navigation marks. Where these are found on other waterways they generally conform to the conventional system of lateral buoyage in tidal waters: red buoys or beacons showing red lights at night being left to port when heading *upstream*, and green buoys or beacons showing green lights at night to starboard (*Fig 1*). (Some lateral marks may also have a white band.)

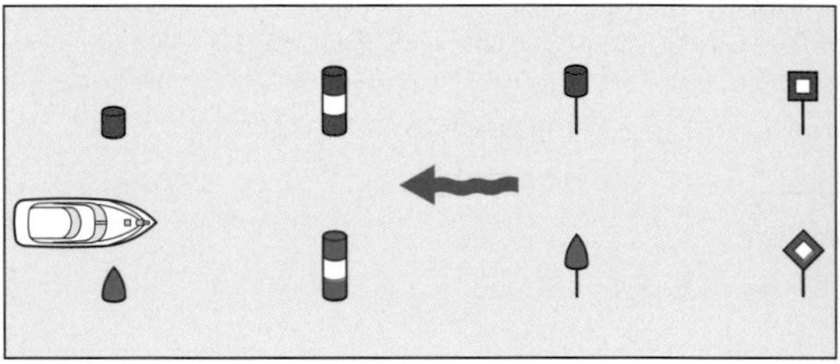

Fig 1

Traffic lights similar to those used on roads are found at some locks and bridges and ***must*** be obeyed (*Fig 2*).

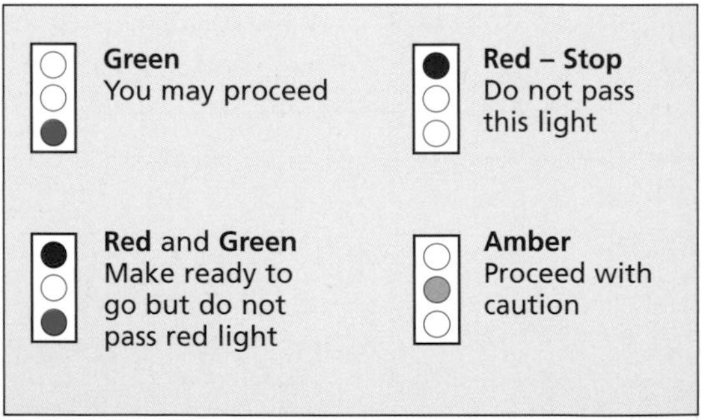

Fig 2

Rules of the Road

In general, boats on inland waterways observe the same rules as seagoing vessels, but as most canals are saucer shaped in section with the deepest water in the middle, whenever possible, you should keep to the middle of the channel except on bends where the deepest water will be on the outside of the bend. Whenever you meet another boat, slow down, move to the right and steer to miss it but do not go in close to the bank or you may run aground.

If you need to overtake another boat, leave it to starboard (*Fig 3*) but do not attempt to overtake near bends, bridges, weirs or locks.

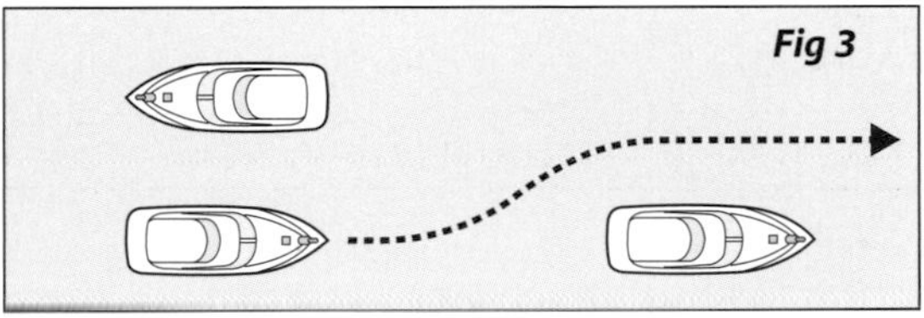

Fig 3

When approaching a bridge where the channel becomes narrower, slow down if a boat coming the other way is nearer to the bridge than you are. Keep over to the right until it is through and clear. On rivers, a boat coming ***downstream*** always has priority (*Fig 4*).

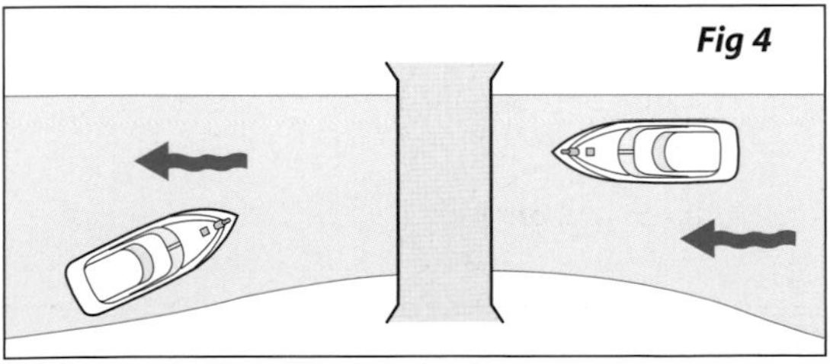

Fig 4

Locks

Locks are set on rivers and canals to enable boats to follow the contours of the land. They vary in both size and design, some being automated, while others are manually operated, but the working principle is the same. Strong gates enclose each end of a brick or stone chamber in which the water level can be adjusted to equal the level above or below the lock.

The water is controlled by sliding 'paddles' which can be opened to let water in at the top end of the lock or out at the bottom. *Ground paddles* control the flow of water through a culvert built into the lock side. *Gate paddles* cover an underwater aperture in the gate itself (*Fig 5*).

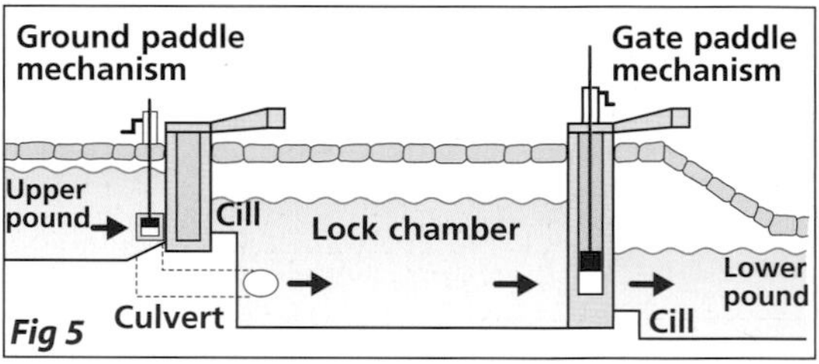

Fig 5

Lock operation The operating procedures are simple – and safe – if carried out correctly.

- A *windlass* is necessary to turn the gear which winds the paddles up or down.
- Make sure that it fits correctly; don't use a square section windlass on a tapered pinion.
- Never leave the windlass on a raised paddle. If the ratchet slips, the windlass will fly off and could seriously injure someone.
- Except in emergencies, always wind the paddle down. Do not release the pawl and let the paddle drop.

Lock dimensions Lengths vary. Width inside:
Narrow locks – 7ft (2m); Broad locks – 14ft (4m) (max).

Going up

1 If the lock is full, ensure that the top paddles are closed. Raise bottom paddles to empty the lock.

2 Open bottom gates and enter the lock. Close the gates and bottom paddles (*Fig 6*).

3 Raise the top paddles and when the lock is full, open the top gates and exit the lock.

4 Close the gates and top paddles.

Fig 6

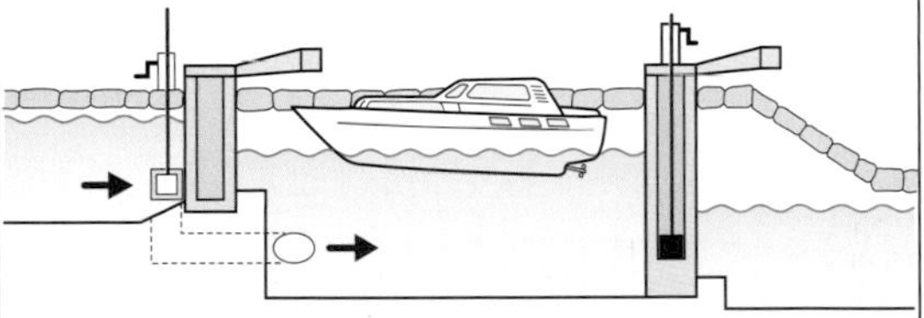

In narrow locks open the paddles gradually. A sudden inrush of water will cause the boat to surge forward violently against the top gate. Hold a cruiser back with ropes around a bollard. Ensure that the rising boat does not become caught under any projections.

If yours is the only boat in a broad lock, open the ground paddle on the same side as the boat first. The inrush of water from the culvert will pin the boat alongside and stop it being washed about.

In locks which have both ground and gate paddles, open the ground paddles first and wait until the water level has risen to cover the gate paddles before you open them. If you open the gate paddles first, you could swamp your boat.

Locks

Going down

1 If the lock is empty, ensure that bottom gates and paddles are closed and raise the top paddles to fill the lock.

2 Open the top gates and enter the lock. Close the gates and the top paddles (*Fig 7*).

3 Raise the bottom paddles and when the lock is empty, open the gates and exit the lock.

4 Close the gates and bottom paddles.

Fig 7

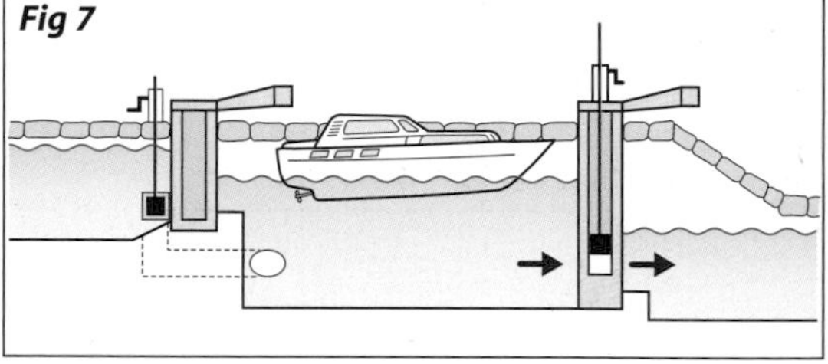

Hold the boat steady with ropes but do not tie them to anything. Ensure that the stern does not settle on to the top gate cill or the bows become hooked on the bottom gate. Some locks taper slightly – ensure that any large pieces of debris, logs etc. do not become wedged between the hull and the lock wall.

▸▸ Man overboard in a lock

IMMEDIATELY close all paddles. Throw a lifebuoy and line, stop the boat engine and ensure that the boat cannot swing and crush the person in the water. (Method of recovery must depend upon circumstances of course.)

Signals

Use your horn to signal your intentions

Short blast ●   *Long blast* ▬   *Pause* ······

●	I am turning to starboard
●●	I am turning to port
●●●	I am going astern
▬ ●●	I am unable to manoeuvre
●●●● ······ ●	I am turning *around* to my right
●●●● ······ ●●	I am turning *around* to my left
●●●●●	Your intentions are unclear

Sound one long blast when approaching blind bends or bridges. Repeat after 20 seconds.

Some common British Waterways signs

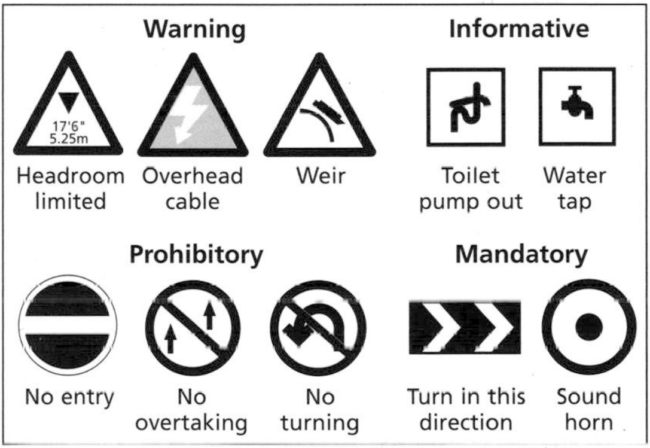

> **▶▶ Note**
> Other navigation authorities may have different signs and regulations. Make sure that you obtain and read a copy of the relevant rules and regulations before you set off.

CEVNI – Rules, regulations & definitions

The *Code Européen des Voies de la Navigation Intérieure* – CEVNI for short – is the code that is used to govern navigation on all the interconnected inland waterways of Europe. The rules, signs, signals and procedures that make up the code are understood, and used by boat-masters of all nationalities and if you intend to visit these waters, you need to have a CEVNI qualification and a good working knowledge of the code to navigate there in safety.

CEVNI classifies vessels over 20m long as 'normal vessels' and gives them priority over small craft, so it is essential for the skipper of a small pleasure craft to understand the intentions of 'normal vessels' and be able to interpret and correctly react to the signs and signals which may be given by them.

Normal vessels going downstream have priority over those coming upstream but upstream vessels can choose which side they will give way on. If the meeting is to be 'port to port' the upstream vessel will make no signal, but if the meeting is to be 'starboard to starboard', the upstream vessel will display a blue board – with or without a scintillating white light – and the downstream vessel signals acknowledgement by displaying its own blue board.

Vessels flying a red pennant at the bows have priority of passage at specified places such as locks – even if they are small craft. They include 'official' boats and those giving a regular passenger service.

Vessels displaying blue cones by day or blue lights at night have dangerous cargoes. Do not attempt to enter a lock with a vessel displaying 2 or 3 blue cones.

▸▸ Note

This section does *not* cover all the rules and signs for CEVNI. It is a legal requirement to carry a copy of the CEVNI handbook on board.

Signals indicating side to pass

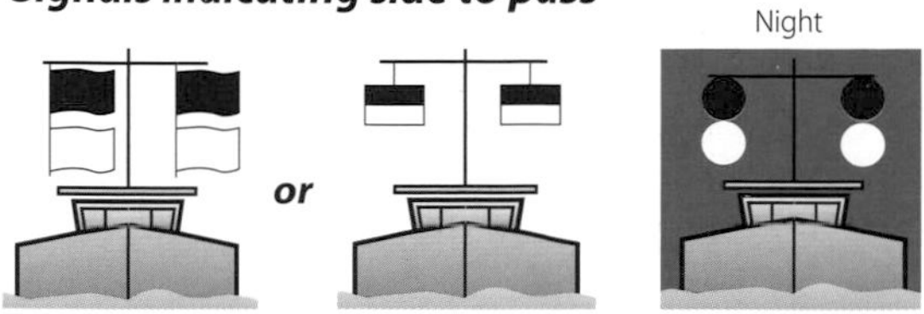

Pass slowly on either side. **DO NOT CREATE WASH.**

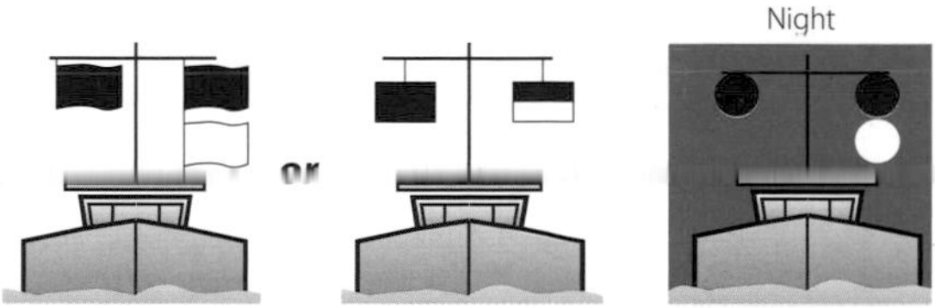

Pass only on the side displaying red and white flags or a red and white board. **DO NOT CREATE WASH.**

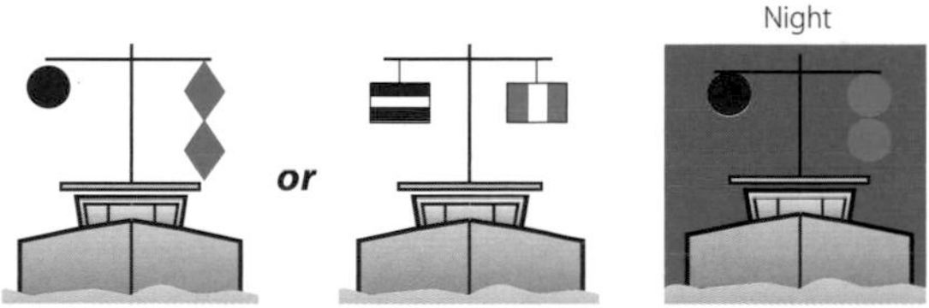

Pass only on the side displaying green bi-cones or a green and white board.

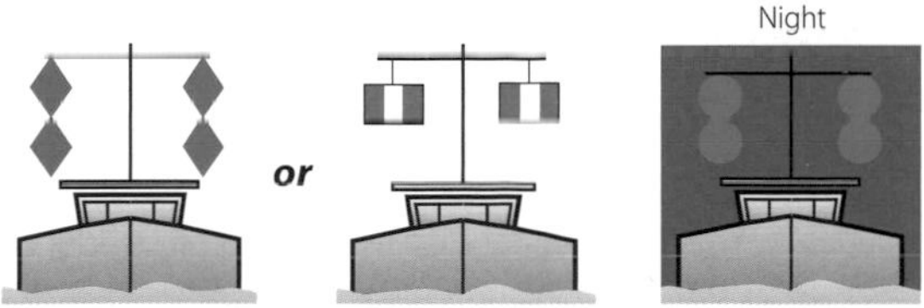

It is safe to pass on either side.

▶▶ Caution

Do not confuse the passage-prohibited sign  with the sign  which permits passage without creating wash.

CEVNI – red waterway signs

General prohibitory signs

ENTRY OR PASSAGE FORBIDDEN

NO ACCESS EXCEPT FOR NON MOTORISED SMALL CRAFT

Specific prohibitions – *Red diagonal bar*

NO OVERTAKING

NO PASSING OR OVERTAKING

NO TURNING

NO ANCHORING

NO MOORING

NO BERTHING

NO MOTORISED VESSELS

NO ROWING BOATS OR CANOES

NO SAILING

Mandatory – *Prescribed course*

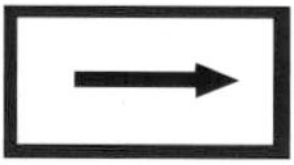
GO IN DIRECTION OF ARROW

MOVE TO LEFT OF CHANNEL

MOVE TO RIGHT OF CHANNEL

KEEP TO LEFT OF CHANNEL

KEEP TO RIGHT OF CHANNEL

CROSS CHANNEL TO PORT

CROSS CHANNEL TO STBD

▸▸ Important

These abridged notes and illustrations should only be used in conjunction with those given in the official CEVNI handbook.

CEVNI – red waterway signs

Restrictions and mandatory instructions

DEPTH LIMIT (190cm)

HEADROOM LIMITED (6m)

PASSAGE CHANNEL WIDTH (18m)

CHANNEL 12m FROM BANK

SPEED LIMIT (6kph

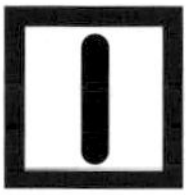

KEEP A SHARP LOOK OUT

STOP AS NECESSARY

SOUND HORN

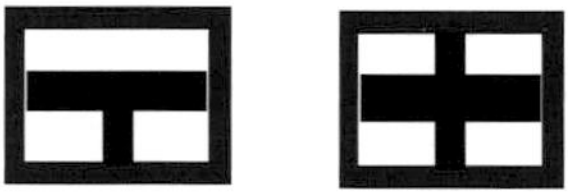

GIVE WAY TO VESSELS USING MAJOR WATERWAY AHEAD

NAVIGATION RESTRICTED MAKE ENQUIRIES

Additional information panels

SPEED LIMIT 8kph IN 500m

BEWARE – FERRY AHEAD

STOP – CUSTOMS

NO BERTHING WITHIN 10m

NO ANCHORING FOR NEXT 500m

STRONG CROSS CURRENT – 150m

CEVNI – blue waterway signs

Blue informative and advisory signs

GO THIS WAY

OVERHEAD CABLE

TURNING AREA

UNPOWERED FERRY

END OF RESTRICTION

WEIR AHEAD

CHANNEL IN LOCAL USE

MAJOR WATERWAY AHEAD

ANCHORING PERMITTED

MOORING PERMITTED

BERTHING PERMITTED

PLEASURE CRAFT MOORINGS 1200m AHEAD

BERTHING RESERVED FOR COMMERCIAL VESSELS

Special berthing signs

Vessels displaying blue cones by day or blue lights at night have dangerous cargoes and special berths distinguished by blue triangles are reserved for these vessels.

Do not berth within 10m of a sign with one blue triangle, within 50m of a sign with two triangles, or within 100m of a sign with three triangles.

Light signals at locks and opening bridges

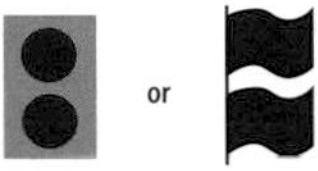

PROLONGED STOPPAGE
(EG LOCK OUT OF SERVICE)

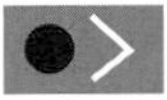

NO ENTRY IN DIRECTION OF
THE ARROW

TEMPORARY STOPPAGE

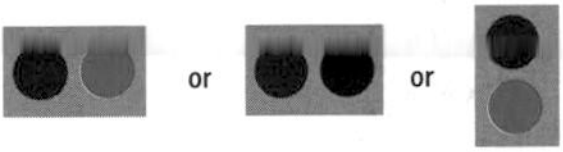

DO NOT PASS – BUT PREPARE TO GET UNDERWAY

Red and green lights control passage under moveable bridges. When yellow lights are shown in conjunction with red lights, passage is permitted for vessels of reduced height.

PASSAGE PERMITTED

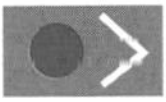

ENTRY PERMITTED
IN DIRECTION OF
THE ARROW

GREEN AND WHITE SIGN
Entry or passage permitted
(May be used in conjunction with lights.)

CEVNI – land marks and cross-overs

Land marks

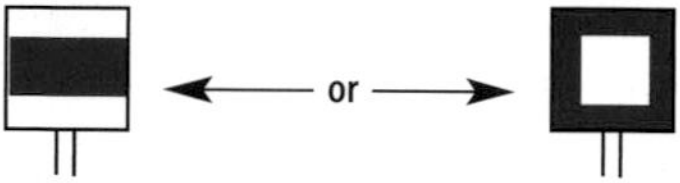

Red and white top marks on posts indicate that the channel lies close to the right bank – the bank on your right-hand side as you travel down stream ('Down hill' on a canal).

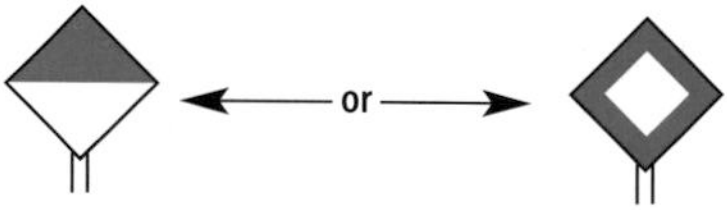

Green and white top marks on posts indicate that the channel lies close to the left bank – the bank on your left-hand side as you travel down stream ('Down hill' on a canal).

Lights – if fitted – are rhythmic red or green as appropriate.

Cross-overs

A post with either a yellow or a yellow and black top mark indicates the place where the channel crosses from one bank to the other.

Lights – when fitted – are yellow. Group flashing (2) or occulting with even number characteristics on the right bank.

Group flashing (3) or occulting with odd number characteristics on the left bank.

CEVNI – fixed bridge markings

Bridges with channels too narrow to allow the simultaneous passage of two or more vessels are marked with either red and white or green and white diamonds.

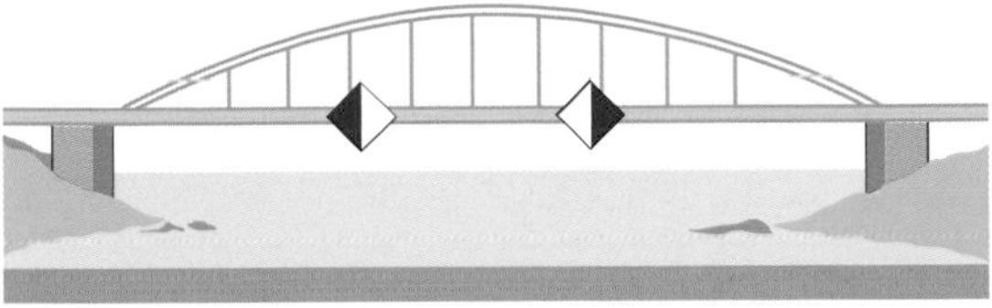

Fig 1 Passage is* PROHIBITED *in the area outside the white triangles.

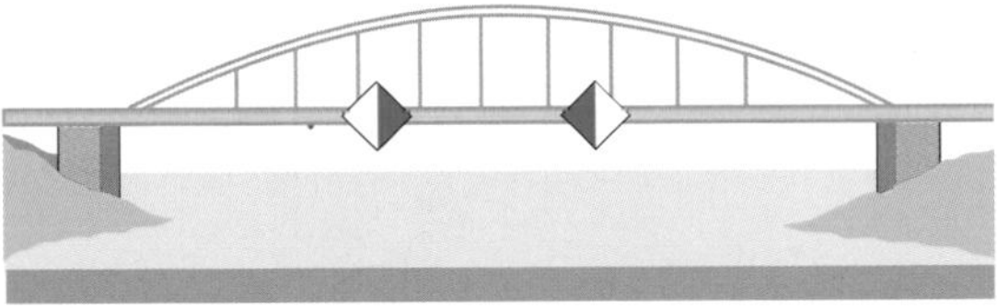

Fig 2 It is* RECOMMENDED *that vessels remain within the area between the green triangles.

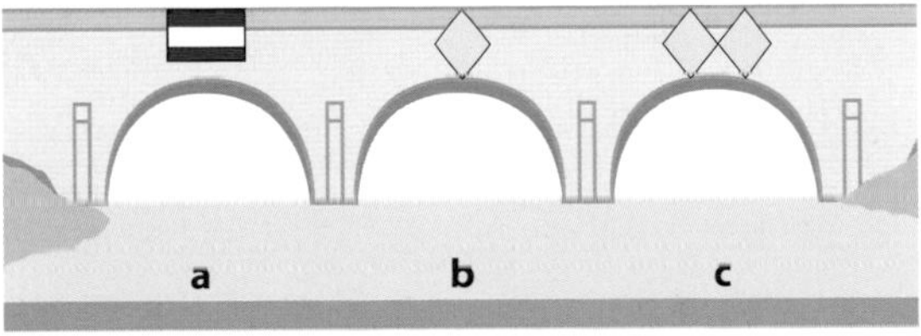

Fig 3a Red and white No entry/No passage sign. The span is closed to traffic travelling in this direction
Fig 3b A single yellow diamond. The recommended route for all vessels. The span is open to traffic in* BOTH *directions.
Fig 3c Two yellow diamonds. The span is open for vessels travelling in this direction, but is closed to vessels coming the other way.

Measured distance

All patent logs should be checked periodically for accuracy. At a number of places on the coast, marks have been set up in transit with accurately measured distances between them to enable the speed of vessels on passage to be checked (*Fig 1*).

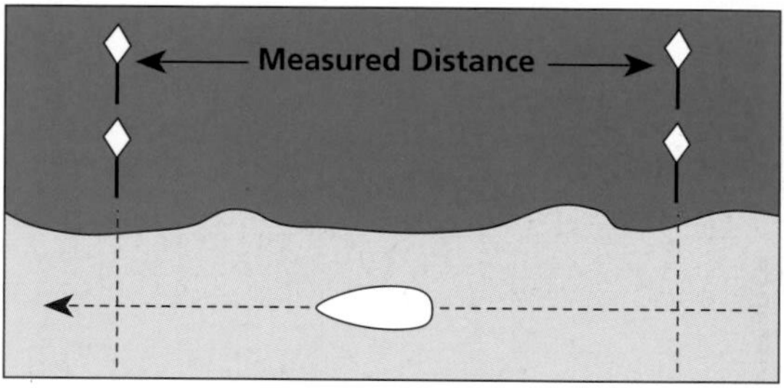

Fig 1

Using any charted distance of any length, steer a course at constant speed under power parallel to the chosen measured distance. Begin timing by stopwatch as the first pair of marks come into transit and stop timing at the second transit.

With only a single run past the marks, allowance must be made for any tidal stream which may be affecting the course. Tidal stream can be ignored, however, when test runs are made at identical speeds in alternate directions. In practice, when checking speed in this manner, it is customary to make two or more runs in each direction to obtain an average speed which is more dependable.

The speed of the vessel over the ground is found by dividing the distance run by the time taken.

To check the accuracy of the log against a measured distance

For each run made, record:

- ◆ *Speed indicated by the log*
- ◆ *Distance recorded by the log*
- ◆ *Actual time taken*

Complete the boxes below and compare the total distance recorded by the log for runs 1 and 2 against the measured distance to obtain the log error. Compare the average speed found against the log's recorded speed to find the log error.

	Distance in metres				Elapsed time in seconds				Speed in knots
Run 1		x	*3600*	÷		÷	*1852*	=	
Run 2		x	*3600*	÷		÷	*1852*	=	

Difference runs 1–2		Approx rate tidal stream
	÷ 2 =	

	Speed in knots			
Total 1 + 2		÷ 2 =		→ Average speed

3600 seconds per hour
1852 metres in one nautical mile

Times, speed, distance/ETA/Tidal stream

Time, speed, distance

$$\frac{\text{Distance x 60}}{\text{Speed}} = \textit{Time} \text{ (in minutes)}$$

$$\frac{\text{Distance x 60}}{\text{Time}} = \textit{Speed} \text{ (in knots)}$$

$$\frac{\text{Speed x Time}}{60} = \textit{Distance} \text{ (in nautical miles)}$$

Estimated Time of Arrival (ETA)

Distance to go x 60 ÷ effective speed

= *Time in minutes*

Add to departure time to obtain *ETA*

A rough estimate of boat speed can be obtained by noting the time it takes to travel its own length past a stationary object in the water.

$$\textit{Speed in knots} = \frac{\text{Length in metres}}{\text{Time in seconds}} \times 1.94$$

OR

$$\textit{Speed in knots} = \frac{\text{Length in feet}}{\text{Time in seconds}} \times 0.59$$

Tidal stream – computation of rate

$$\frac{\text{Range of tide for day}}{\text{Spring range of tide}} \times \text{ Spring rate of tidal stream}$$

Distance off/Conversion/Sun movement

Distance off by vertical sextant angle

$$\text{Dist Off (n miles)} = \frac{1.852 \times \text{ht in metres}}{\text{angle in mins of arc}}$$

Distance of visible horizon (n miles):
$\sqrt{\text{Ht of eye (metres)}} \times 2.075$

One nautical mile	=	1·852 kilometres
	=	1·15078 statute miles
	=	6076·12 feet
	=	1852 metres
	=	10 cables

Conversion factors

Feet to metres	multiply by	0·3048
Metres to feet	"	3·2808
N miles to statute miles	"	1·1515
Statute miles to n miles	"	0·8684
Knots to mph	"	1·1515
Mph to knots	"	0·8684
Knots to km/hr	"	1·8519
Km/hr to knots	"	0·5400
Sq ft to sq m	"	0·0929
Sq m to sq ft	"	10·7643
Litres to pints	"	1.7600
Litres to gallons	"	0.2200
Pints to litres	"	0.5683
Gallons to litres	"	4.5460

1 Gallon (English)	=	4.546 litres
1 Gallon (USA)	=	3.785 litres

Apparent movement of the sun

1° in 4 mins
15° in 1 hour
360° in 24 hours

Distance off by vertical angle

Dist in miles	Height in metres									
	10	20	30	40	50	60	70	80	90	100
	Vertical angle									
0.1	3° 05′	6° 10′	9° 12′	12° 11′	15° 06′	17° 56′	20° 42′	23° 21′	25° 54′	28° 21′
0.2	1 33	3 05	4 38	6 10	7 41	9 12	10 42	12 11	13 39	15 06
0.3	1 02	2 04	3 05	4 07	5 08	6 10	7 11	8 11	9 12	10 12
0.4	0 46	1 33	2 19	3 05	3 52	4 38	5 24	6 10	6 55	7 41
0.5	0 37	1 14	1 51	2 28	3 05	3 42	4 19	4 56	5 33	6 10
0.6	0 31	1 02	1 33	2 04	2 34	3 05	3 36	4 07	4 38	5 08
0.7	0 27	0 53	1 19	1 46	2 12	2 39	3 05	3 32	3 58	4 24
0.8	0 23	0 46	1 10	1 33	1 56	2 19	2 42	3 05	3 28	3 52
0.9	0 21	0 41	1 02	1 22	1 43	2 04	2 24	2 45	3 05	3 26
1.0	0 19	0 37	0 56	1 14	1 33	1 51	2 10	2 28	2 47	3 05
1.1	0 17	0 34	0 51	1 07	1 24	1 41	1 58	2 15	2 32	2 49
1.2	0 15	0 31	0 46	1 02	1 17	1 33	1 48	2 04	2 19	2 34
1.3	0 14	0 29	0 43	0 57	1 11	1 26	1 40	1 54	2 08	2 23
1.4	0 13	0 27	0 40	0 53	1 06	1 19	1 33	1 46	1 59	2 12
1.5	0 12	0 25	0 37	0 49	1 02	1 14	1 27	1 39	1 51	2 04
1.6	0 12	0 23	0 35	0 46	0 58	1 10	1 21	1 33	1 44	1 56
1.7	0 11	0 22	0 33	0 44	0 55	1 05	1 16	1 27	1 38	1 49
1.8	0 10	0 21	0 31	0 41	0 52	1 02	1 12	1 22	1 33	1 43
1.9	0 10	0 20	0 29	0 39	0 49	0 59	1 08	1 18	1 28	1 38
2.0	0 09	0 19	0 28	0 37	0 46	0 56	1 05	1 14	1 23	1 33
2.1	0 09	0 18	0 27	0 35	0 44	0 53	1 02	1 11	1 19	1 28
2.2	0 08	0 17	0 25	0 34	0 42	0 51	0 59	1 07	1 16	1 24
2.3	0 08	0 16	0 24	0 32	0 40	0 48	0 56	1 05	1 13	1 21
2.4	0 08	0 15	0 23	0 31	0 39	0 46	0 54	1 02	1 10	1 17
2.5	0 07	0 15	0 22	0 30	0 37	0 45	0 52	0 59	1 07	1 14
2.6	0 07	0 14	0 21	0 29	0 36	0 43	0 50	0 57	1 04	1 11
2.7	0 07	0 14	0 21	0 27	0 34	0 41	0 48	0 55	1 02	1 09
2.8	0 07	0 13	0 20	0 27	0 33	0 40	0 46	0 53	1 00	1 06
2.9	0 06	0 13	0 19	0 26	0 32	0 38	0 45	0 51	0 58	1 04
3.0	0 06	0 12	0 19	0 25	0 31	0 37	0 43	0 49	0 56	1 02
3.1	0 06	0 12	0 18	0 24	0 30	0 36	0 42	0 48	0 54	1 00
3.2	0 06	0 12	0 17	0 23	0 29	0 35	0 41	0 46	0 52	0 58
3.3	0 06	0 11	0 17	0 22	0 28	0 34	0 39	0 45	0 51	0 56
3.4	0 05	0 11	0 16	0 22	0 27	0 33	0 38	0 44	0 49	0 55
3.5	0 05	0 11	0 16	0 21	0 27	0 32	0 37	0 42	0 48	0 53
3.6	0 05	0 10	0 15	0 21	0 26	0 31	0 35	0 41	0 46	0 52
3.7	0 05	0 10	0 15	0 20	0 25	0 30	0 35	0 40	0 45	0 50
3.8	0 05	0 10	0 15	0 20	0 24	0 29	0 34	0 39	0 44	0 49
3.9	0 05	0 10	0 14	0 19	0 24	0 29	0 33	0 38	0 43	0 48
4.0	0 05	0 09	0 14	0 19	0 23	0 28	0 32	0 37	0 42	0 46
4.1	0 05	0 09	0 14	0 18	0 23	0 27	0 32	0 35	0 41	0 45
4.2	0 04	0 09	0 13	0 18	0 22	0 27	0 31	0 35	0 40	0 44
4.3	0 04	0 09	0 13	0 17	0 22	0 26	0 30	0 35	0 39	0 43
4.4	0 04	0 08	0 13	0 17	0 21	0 25	0 30	0 34	0 38	0 42
4.5	0 04	0 08	0 12	0 16	0 21	0 24	0 29	0 33	0 37	0 41
4.6	0 04	0 08	0 12	0 16	0 20	0 24	0 28	0 32	0 36	0 40
4.7	0 04	0 08	0 12	0 16	0 20	0 24	0 28	0 32	0 36	0 39
4.8	0 04	0 08	0 12	0 15	0 19	0 23	0 27	0 31	0 35	0 39
4.9	0 04	0 08	0 11	0 15	0 19	0 23	0 27	0 30	0 34	0 38
5.0	0 04	0 07	0 11	0 15	0 19	0 22	0 25	0 30	0 33	0 37
	32.8	65.6	98.41	31.2	164.0	196.8	229.7	262.5	295.3	328.1
	Height in feet									

See page 96

Distance of lights – rising or dipping

Height of Light		HEIGHT OF EYE				
		Metres				
		1.5	3	4.6	6.1	7.6
		Feet				
		5	10	15	20	25
m	ft					
12	40	9¾	11	11¾	12½	13
15	50	10¾	11¾	12½	13¼	14
18	60	11½	12½	13½	14	14¾
21	70	12¼	13¼	14	14¾	15½
24	80	13	14	14¾	15½	16
27	90	13½	14½	15½	16	16¾
30	100	14	15	16	16½	17¼
34	110	14½	15¾	16½	17¼	17¾
37	120	15¼	16¼	17	17¾	18¼
40	130	15¾	16¾	17½	18¼	19
43	140	16¼	17¼	18	18¾	19½
46	150	16¾	17¾	18½	19¼	19¾
49	160	17	18¼	19	19¾	20¼
52	170	17½	18½	19½	20	20¾
55	180	18	19	20	20½	21¼
58	190	18½	19½	20¼	21	21½
61	200	18¾	20	20¾	21½	22
64	210	19¼	20¼	21	21¾	22½
67	220	19½	20¾	21½	22¼	22¾
70	230	20	21	22	22½	23¼
73	240	20½	21½	22¼	23	23½
76	250	20¾	21¾	22½	23¼	24
79	260	21	22¼	23	23¾	24¼
82	270	21½	22½	23¼	24	24½
85	280	21¾	23	23¾	24½	25
88	290	22	23¼	24	24¾	25¼
91	300	22½	23½	24½	25	25¾

Distance of sea horizon

Height of eye metres	feet	Distance n miles	Height of eye metres	feet	Distance n miles
0.3	1	1.15	4.3	14	4.30
0.6	2	1.62	4.9	16	4.60
0.9	3	1.99	5.5	18	4.87
1.2	4	2.30	6.1	20	5.14
1.5	5	2.57	6.7	22	5.39
1.8	6	2.81	7.3	24	5.62
2.1	7	3.04	7.9	26	5.86
2.4	8	3.25	8.5	28	6.08
2.7	9	3.45	9.1	30	6.30
3.0	10	3.63	9.8	32	6.50
3.4	11	3.81	10.4	34	6.70
3.7	12	3.98	11.0	36	6.90
4.0	13	4.14	11.6	38	7.09

Index

Index

Index